Catholic Bible Study

The Gospel of Matthew

by

Father Joseph L. Ponessa, S.S.D.

and

Laurie Watson Manhardt, Ph.D.

Emmaus Road Publishing
1468 Parkview Circle
Steubenville, OH 43952

All rights reserved. Published in 2016
Printed in the United States of America

Library of Congress Control Number: 2016953068
ISBN: 9781945125041

Cover design and layout by
Jacinta Calcut, Image Graphics & Design, www.image–gd.com

Cover artwork:
Melissa Dayton, *The Sermon on the Mount*

Nihil obstat: Reverend Jose Valliparambil, STD, *Censor Deputatis*

Imprimatur: Most Reverend Michael William Warfel,
Bishop of Great Falls and Billings, May 1, 2016

The *nihil obstat* and *imprimatur* are official declarations that a work is considered to be free from doctrinal or moral error. It is not implied that those who have granted the same agree with the content, opinions, or statements expressed.

For additional information on the "Come and See~ Catholic Bible Study" series visit www.CatholicBibleStudy.net

Catholic Bible Study

The Gospel of Matthew

Introduction

Come to me, all who labor and are heavy laden, and I will give you rest.
Take my yoke upon you, and learn from me;
for I am gently and lowly in heart, and you will find rest for your souls.
For my yoke is easy, and my burden is light.
Matthew 11:28–30

The Gospel of Matthew—gives readers an invitation to repent and believe in Jesus, the Son of David, who fulfills God's promise of a Redeemer for fallen humanity. Jesus satisfies the Old Testament prophecies pointing to a Messiah for Israel and a Savior for sinners. Matthew uses more Old Testament references than any other Gospel writer. Jesus inaugurates the *kingdom of God* on earth and invites believers into His kingdom. Meet the King of Kings and share the good news with others.

Matthew (Levi, son of Alphaeus), the Jewish tax collector, writes primarily for Jewish readers, presuming their knowledge of Hebrew Scriptures, traditions, and idioms. He presents Jesus of Nazareth as the long-awaited Messiah of Israel, the King of the Jews, establishing the Kingdom of God on earth. Jesus, the Great Teacher, demonstrates and instructs disciples on how to live in His kingdom.

Of all four evangelists, only Matthew identifies the Church and primacy of Peter. Two apostles, James, son of Alphaeus, and Levi, son of Alphaeus, (Mark 2:14; 10:3), may have been brothers. The martyrdom of James, son of Zebedee by Herod (Acts 12:2) precipitated the writing of the Gospel of Mark around the year AD 50. Josephus indicates that James, son of Alphaeus was the second apostle martyred, which may have triggered the writing of the Gospel of Matthew around AD 60, or at some time around the destruction of Jerusalem in AD 70.

Jesus' five major discourses or sermons provide the structure of Matthew's Gospel. These familiar teachings can be identified as follows:
+ The Sermon on the Mount (Matthew 5–7)
+ Missionary Discourse (Matthew 10)
+ Kingdom Parables (Matthew 13)
+ Discipleship/Church Discourse (Matthew 18)
+ Apocalyptic Judgment Sermon (Matthew 23–25)

The Gospel of Matthew highlights the Kingdom of God. The word "kingdom" appears over fifty times in this gospel. Jesus says, *"Repent, for the kingdom of heaven is at hand"* (Matthew 4:17). The kingdom of God is among you, for where Jesus is there is the kingdom. Jesus establishes His kingdom on earth in His Church, where He remains until the end of the age. He commands the apostles to proclaim the good news to all the earth. Then, Jesus promises to bring His faithful servants with Him into His kingdom in heaven, when He comes again in power and glory to judge the living and the dead (Matthew 24).

What You Need

In order to do this Bible Study, you will need a Catholic Bible and the Catechism of the Catholic Church (CCC). The Catechism can be easily accessed on the Internet:
http://www.vatican.va/archive/ENG0015/_INDEX.HTM

Remember that the Catholic Bible has seventy-three books. The Council of Hippo approved these seventy-three books in AD 393. The Council of Trent in AD 1546 reaffirmed these divinely inspired books as the canon of the Bible.

For Bible Study purposes, choose a word-for-word, literal translation rather than a paraphrase of the Bible. An excellent English translation is the Revised Standard Version Catholic Edition (RSVCE) Bible. **Because of different verse numbering in various Bible translations, the RSVCE second edition by Ignatius Press will be the easiest to consult to complete the home study questions in the *Come and See ~ Catholic Bible Study* series.**

How To Do This Bible Study

1. Pray to the Holy Spirit to enlighten your mind and spirit.
2. Read the Bible passages and commentary in this book for the first chapter.
3. Use your Bible and Catechism to write answers to the home study questions.
4. Put your answers in your own words in a short phrase or sentence.
5. Watch the videotape lecture that goes with this study.
6. In a small group, share your answers aloud on those questions.

There is only one God, brethren, and we learn about Him only from Sacred Scripture. It is therefore our duty to become acquainted with what Scripture proclaims and to investigate its teachings thoroughly. We should believe them in the sense that the Father wills, thinking of the Son in the way the Father wills, and accepting the teaching He wills to give us with regard to the Holy Spirit.

Sacred Scripture is God's gift to us and it should be understood in the way that He intends. We should not do violence to it by interpreting it according to our own preconceived ideas.

Saint Hipploytus (AD 170–236), *Treatise Against the Heresy of Noetus*, 9.

A Prayer to the Holy Spirit

O Holy Spirit, Beloved of my soul, I adore You,
enlighten, guide, strengthen, and console me.
Tell me what I ought to say and do, and command me to do it.
I promise to be submissive in everything You will ask of me,
and to accept all that You permit to happen to me,
only show me what is Your will.
Amen.

Chapter 1

The Birth of Jesus
Matthew 1

Behold, an angel of the Lord appeared to him [Joseph] in a dream, saying,
"Joseph, son of David, do not fear to take Mary your wife,
for that which is conceived in her is of the Holy Spirit;
she will bear a son, and you shall call his name Jesus,
for he will save his people from their sins.
Matthew 1:20–21

The Genealogy of Jesus—In contemporary society, with birth certificates, hospital records, driver's licenses and passports, paper and electronic documents confirm one's identity. In antiquity, however, the oral genealogic record fixed in a person's mind his family lineage and identity. Genealogies answered a number of critical questions. Who are you? From where have you come? Who are your people? In cultures in which only a select few people could read and had access to writing implements, the oral recollection of one's ancestry was essential.

Each Advent, millions of Catholics around the world hear the genealogy of Jesus Christ read on December 17th and again on Christmas. Like Genesis, Matthew gives a new beginning and recapitulates the history of ancient Israel. Immediately, Matthew introduces *Jesus Christ, the son of David, the son of Abraham* (Matthew 1:1). *Jesus* is the Greek form of the Hebrew name *Yeshua* or Joshua, meaning "Savior," or "God saves." Originally, the literal translation begged, "God help!" *Christ,* the Greek form of "Messiah," means "Anointed One." In this way, Matthew announces that Jesus, the son of David, fulfills Israel's hope for a long-awaited Messiah King. Jesus, the royal king, is identified as *the son of David* in all the major writings of the New Testament, except the Letter to the Hebrews.

In the first line of this Gospel, Matthew highlights King David first, even though he came long after his ancestor, Abraham. King David's importance can be shown by the fact that David's name appears over one thousand times in the Bible, and six times in this chapter alone (Matthew 1:1, 5, 6, 17 twice, 20). God's covenants with Abraham *"I will make of you a great nation, and I will bless you, and make your name great, so that you will be a blessing . . . and by you all the families of the earth shall bless themselves"* (Genesis 12:2–3), and David *"And your house and your kingdom shall be made sure for ever before me; your throne shall be established for ever"* (2 Samuel 7:16), are both fulfilled in Jesus Christ.

Listing Jesus as a descendant of Abraham shows that Jesus, a true Israelite, belongs to the chosen people. King David is the only person in the genealogy other than Jesus Christ, who claims an identifying title of honor. The reader sees that Jesus Christ is the Messiah "King of the Jews," which will also appear on His Cross.

Sixteen verses of Scripture (Matthew 1:1–16) outline the overall history of Israel in three major segments. Matthew provides a schematic arrangement, highlighting the important names, while purposely omitting three immoral, apostate kings from the last segment. Despite the omission of these names, Matthew cannot be accused of sugar coating the ancestry of Jesus, since a number of despicable characters emerge. Following King David, there were a number of wicked kings, including Rehoboam, Abijah, Joram, Ahaz and Manasseh. *Manasseh seduced them to do more evil than the nations had done whom the* LORD *destroyed before the sons of Israel. . . . Moreover Manasseh shed very much innocent blood* (2 Kings 21:9, 16). The three periods of Israel's history could be outlined as follows.

Periods of Israel's History

Pre-monarch period	Abraham to King David	Matthew 1:2–6a
Monarchy	David to Babylonian Exile	Matthew 1:6b–11
Collapse of Monarchy	Exile (586 BC) to Jesus	Matthew 1:12–16

Israel's history, like many other nations, reveals peaks and valleys. Times of great glory, as in the days of King David and his conquests, precede times of ruin, as in the Babylonian exile. For the most part, good times follow when Israel obeys the commandments of God. Rebellion and disobedience usually result in times of adversity. The history of Israel follows a cyclical pattern of obedience and prosperity, followed by disobedience and adversity, and then turning back to God.

A similar pattern can be found in people as in nations. Often, a person begins with a close relationship with God in childhood. Temptations come and a person may fall into disobedience or even rebellion. Sin is often its own punishment. When a person hits the bottom of his barrel, he may cry out to God, who is rich in mercy and ready to forgive and offer second chances. Nations can follow the same sad pattern of rebellion, repentance—turning back to God, and sinning again.

If there are imperfect people in your family history, you can identify with Jesus. Several sinful people appear in the genealogy of Jesus. Anyone can try to overcome the legacy of one's family background. Prayer can be a powerful tool in breaking family patterns of sin and weakness, and developing virtues instead. A priest or prayer partner can help identify evil strongholds and ask God to break them.

Biblical genealogies usually include only masculine names in the family lineage. *Abraham was the father of Isaac, and Isaac the father of Jacob, and Jacob the father of Judah and his brothers* (Matthew 1:2). Mothers and daughters are seldom mentioned. However, in the genealogy of Jesus Christ, five women's names appear. Some of these women are Gentiles in irregular situations, and only one woman is pure and Jewish. Pope Benedict XVI explains the curious inclusion of these unique women.

There was indeed a tradition of emphasizing four women in the history of Israel as the great ancestresses: Sarah, Rebekah, Leah, and Rachel. However, Matthew mentions, not these four, but four others—four women who were somewhat embarrassing figures, women who disturbed the purity of a genealogy and were considered blemishes on the history of Israel. That is why people tended to pass over these women in silence.

Some scholars have suggested that Matthew is pointing in his genealogy of Jesus to something he intended to make the underlying leitmotif of his entire Gospel: that the last shall be the first. Human criteria are overturned by God. God has chosen that which is weak. And since all these four women are sinners, the mention of their names makes the genealogy a genealogy of grace that welcomes the sinner and that is based on forgiveness, not on human greatness or achievements.

All this is true, but I believe that it does not do justice to the central perspective Matthew intended. If we look more closely, we will see that the sin involved in all four Old Testament narratives was the sin of a man, not the sin of a woman! The specific point about these four women is that they were not Jewish. It was precisely these Gentile women who appeared on the scene at decisive turning points in the history of Israel, and this is why they may rightly be considered the real ancestresses of the kingdom in Israel. . . . It is the women who are the real hinges on which the genealogy turns. Instead of a genealogy of supposedly male deeds, it becomes a genealogy of faith and grace. The real heart of this history, the continuing story of God's promise, is based on the faith of these women.

Despite all the differences, we can see an inherent connection here to the fifth woman, in whom the genealogy reaches its culmination: Mary. . . . Up to now, the individual names are always linked by the phrase "was the father of". But at the close of the genealogy, we hear nothing about "begetting". We are told: "Jacob was the father of Joseph, the husband of Mary, of whom Jesus was born, who is called Christ." Joseph was not the father of Jesus: he was only the husband of Mary. It is only through the bridge of this legal belonging, not by means of a biological link, that Jesus belongs to this genealogy and the genealogy to him. He is the legal and legitimate possessor of the genealogy; for Israel, the legal origin, not the biological origin, was always the decisive point, the real heart of the matter. Thanks to the bridge of this law, the Old Testament belongs to Jesus.

At the same time, a new beginning is made. This true beginning that determines everything takes place through faith—through Mary's *fiat*. This true beginning is prefigured and anticipated in something that again and again led to an effective beginning in Israel: the faith of mothers, the faith of foreigners.

Pope Benedict XVI, *The Blessing of Christmas,*
(San Francisco: Ignatius Press, 2007), 40–49

The Birth of Jesus Christ—Matthew relates the birth of Jesus from the perspective of Joseph. Names were very important in ancient Israel. The name "Joseph" would immediately bring to a Jewish person's mind the Old Testament Joseph, beloved son of Jacob and Rachel. A number of similarities can be found between the Old Testament Joseph and the New Testament Joseph, husband of Mary.

Old Testament Joseph	New Testament Joseph
Father's name—Jacob (Genesis 30:1ff).	Father's name—Jacob (Matthew 1:16).
Joseph is a dreamer (Genesis 37:5–11).	An angel appears to Joseph in a dream (Matthew 1:20).
Joseph resists sexual temptations (Genesis 39:7ff).	Joseph was a just and chaste man (Matthew 1:19, 25).
Joseph saves his family from starving by bringing them to Egypt (Genesis 45–46).	Joseph saves the Holy Child from death, by bringing Jesus and Mary to Egypt (Matthew 2:13–15).

Betrothal in ancient Israel was a formal, legally binding, religious rite. Once a man and woman were betrothed, they were considered legally married, and only death or divorce could break their bond. After betrothal, the man would go back to prepare a home for his wife and return later to bring her to his home to live with him. Joseph and Mary are in the midst of this betrothal period when Joseph learns that Mary is with child. It is impossible to imagine what Joseph might be thinking and feeling at this time—confusion, disappointment, anger, or betrayal?

Now the birth of Jesus Christ took place in this way. When his mother Mary had been betrothed to Joseph, before they came together she was found to be with child of the Holy Spirit; and her husband Joseph, being a just man and unwilling to put her to shame, resolved to send her away quietly (Matthew 1:18–19). Because Joseph is a righteous man, he cannot, in justice, condone the sin of another, or lie about the paternity of a child. Mosaic Law prescribes the severe punishment for adultery very precisely. *"If a man commits adultery with the wife of his neighbor, both the adulterer and the adulteress shall be put to death"* (Leviticus 20:10).

Joseph does not want to see Mary stoned to death. Nor does he want to publicly shame her by going through a public divorce. So, the only seemingly acceptable option open to Joseph appears to be quietly sending her away. But, even while he is contemplating his options, an angel of the Lord appears to him in a dream. *"Joseph, son of David, do not fear to take Mary your wife, for that which is conceived in her is of the Holy Spirit; she will bear a son, and you shall call his name Jesus, for he will save his people from their sins"* (Matthew 1:20–21).

Angels must be fearful beings, for those who see angels in the Bible are terrified and need to be reassured not to fear (Matthew 1:20; Luke 1:13, 30). God reveals the truth that Mary, still a virgin, has conceived by the Holy Spirit. Mary fulfills the Old Testament prophecy that Isaiah gave to King Ahaz: *Behold, a virgin shall conceive and bear a son, and shall call his name Immanu-el* (Isaiah 7:14). Mary is without sin. She has not betrayed Joseph or the terms of their betrothal. Mary is innocent of any wrongdoing that people might assume about her. She needs protection. Mary needs a righteous husband—Joseph.

Obeying the angel's directives given in the dream, Joseph wakes and takes Mary as his wife, *but knew her not until (heos* in Greek*) she had borne a son* (Matthew 1:25). Some people distort this verse to deny the Perpetual Virginity of Mary. The preposition "until" does not imply that something different happened later. In the Old Testament, *Michal the daughter of Saul had no child to (heos) the day of her death* (2 Samuel 6:23). No one would imagine that something different happened *after* her death! And, no siblings appear at the foot of Jesus' Cross to offer support or compassion.

Mary's Perpetual Virginity—Church dogma upholds Mary's perpetual virginity, before, during, and after the birth of Christ. Jesus was Mary's only Son, but her spiritual motherhood extends to all people. The perpetual virginity of Mary in no way denies or demeans the goodness of sexual intimacy, which fulfills God's perfect plan for most people, who embrace the sacrament of matrimony. Rather, Mary's perpetual virginity fulfills the will of God for her, and her unique role in the plan of salvation as the Mother of God. Mary and Joseph enter into a *Josephite marriage,* and forego natural marital relations for the supernatural plan of God.

Usually, God saved Israel from their enemies. Here, the angel proposes a new concept— Jesus will save people from their *sins*. Jesus demonstrates His power to forgive sins and free people from bondage. *"Take heart, my son; your sins are forgiven"* (Matthew 9:2). With many allusions to Old Testament prophecies and specific quotations, Matthew reveals that Jesus does something that fulfills a prophecy. *All this took place to fulfill what the Lord had spoken by the prophet: "Behold, a virgin shall conceive and bear a son, and his name shall be called Emmanuel"* (Matthew 1:22–23). Matthew almost shouts to the Jewish people: "See the Messiah we have long awaited! Jesus Christ fulfills the prophecies!"

Matthew's first chapter closes with Joseph giving his Son the name "Jesus," the name that appears over one hundred times in this Gospel. Jesus' name offers comfort, hope, salvation, and power to believers. Peter instructs, *"Repent, and be baptized every one of you in the name of Jesus Christ for the forgiveness of your sins; and you shall receive the gift of the Holy Spirit"* (Acts 2:38). Paul offers the sublime prayer: *God has highly exalted him and bestowed on him the name which is above every name, that at the name of Jesus every knee should bow . . . and every tongue confess that Jesus Christ is Lord, to the glory of God the Father* (Philippians 2:9–11).

1. How does the Gospel of Matthew begin?

2. How many times does David's name appear in Matthew 1:1–21?

3. What can you learn about these people in the genealogy of Jesus?

Abraham	Genesis 12:1–3
Ruth	Ruth 1:4
David	2 Samuel 7:16
Joseph	Matthew 1:20
Mary	Luke 1:26–31

4. Explain the conception of Jesus.

Matthew 1:18–20
CCC 437
CCC 497

5. Use a dictionary to define "betrothal."

6. What do Catholics believe about the Holy Spirit?

Matthew 1:18, 20
CCC 683
CCC 685–686
CCC 688, 690

7. What type of being appears to both Mary and Joseph?

Luke 1:26ff
Matthew 1:20–21
CCC 148

8. Explain "angels."

CCC 328–329
CCC 330
CCC 331–332

9. People who see angels experience what emotion? Matthew 1:20; Luke 1:29

10. What did Joseph assume when Mary was found to be pregnant? Matthew 1:18

11. What is Joseph's relationship to Mary? Matthew 1:19

12. Mosaic Law imposed what punishment for adultery? Leviticus 20:10

13. What dilemma did Joseph face? Matthew 1:18–19

14. What adjective does the Bible use to describe Joseph? Matthew 1:19

* What adjective might someone use to describe you?

15. What is the significance of the name given to the Child?

Matthew 1:21, 23
Luke 1:35
Luke 2:21
CCC 430, 432, CCC 744

16. What does Saint Paul say about the name of Jesus? Philippians 2:9–11

17. What prophecy does the Blessed Virgin Mary fulfill? Isaiah 7:14

18. How does Joseph respond to his dream? Matthew 1:24

19. Explain the Perpetual Virginity of Mary.

Matthew 1:18–25
CCC 499
CCC 500

20. Why is Mary ever-virgin? What does she symbolize?

CCC 506
CCC 507

* Explain proper Catholic Marian devotion.   CCC 501

CHAPTER 2

The Guiding Star
Matthew 2

Where is he who has been born king of the Jews?
For we have seen his star in the East and have come to worship him.
Matthew 2:2

Matthew tells what happens between the Presentation of Jesus in the Temple (Luke 2:22–38) and the return to Galilee (Luke 2:39; Matthew 2:22). Matthew 2 could easily fall into the middle of Luke's text, immediately after Luke 2:38.

Wise Men from the East came to Jerusalem (Matthew 2:1). Matthew calls them the *magoi*, members of an elite caste of Zoroastrian priests, who acted as imperial tutors under the Persian (550—330 BC) and Parthian Empires (247 BC—AD 224). The Jews knew the Magi as benefactors, who advised the Persian rulers to let the Jews return from exile. In Christian tradition, Caspar, Balthazar, and Melchior represent the entire Gentile world. Nativity scenes depict Caspar as a black king, showing the racial diversity and inclusion of the whole human family. The Magi come now with keen interest in the Jewish monarchy. Matthew's Gospel is framed by the exchange of ambassadors. First, Gentiles send Magi to the infant king; finally, Jesus sends apostles back to them. Magi and apostles are mutual ambassadors between the people of this world and the King of the next.

"For we have seen his star in the East, and have come to worship him" (Matthew 2:2). The Magi saw the star in the Western sky, so the verse should read: "we in the East have seen his star." Ignatius of Antioch gave this description: "A star shone forth in the heavens above all the stars; and its light was indescribable, and its strangeness caused amazement; and all the rest of the constellations with the sun and moon formed themselves into a chorus about the star; but the star itself far outshone them all." Scientists have identified a supernova remnant RCW 86, some 8,000 light years away. God sent the star to the Magi thousands of years ahead of time; the fireworks preceded the royal birthday.

"And you, O Bethlehem, in the land of Judah, are by no means least among the rulers of Judah; for from you shall come a ruler who will govern my people Israel" (Matthew 2:6). This prophecy (Micah 5:2) reaffirms the House of David, who came from this town of Bethlehem (1 Samuel 17:12ff). Herod wanted to hear again the verse that gave him nightmares. Arrogantly, Herod built his great tomb, the Herodion, halfway between Jerusalem and Bethlehem, so relatives of David would have to pass by him all the time. Mary and Joseph had passed the Herodion en route to the census, and probably shuddered at the audacity of the usurper.

The Magi follow the star with great rejoicing. When they find the Child with Mary, they fall down prostrate to worship Him. Note the sound Mariology demonstrated by the wise men. They worship Jesus in the presence of His Blessed Mother. These Gentiles fall prostrate in adoration of the King, offering gifts of gold, frankincense, and myrrh. When the Queen of Sheba met King Solomon, she offered him *very much gold* (1 Kings 10:1–2). Gold reveals Christ's kingship, not just as King of the Jews, but the King of Kings for the whole world. Frankincense, an expensive perfume used in making holy incense for the Lord (Exodus 30:34) reveals Christ's Divinity. Incense is used to worship God. Myrrh, a burial ointment, highlights Christ's humanity, prefiguring Jesus' passion and death.

+ Gold — for the King of Kings
+ Incense — for the One true God, revealing Christ's Divinity
+ Myrrh — for burial, showing Christ's humanity

Just as the Magi see only a poor, small Babe in His Mother's arms, their faith enables them to worship beyond what they can see with their eyes. Similarly, when approaching the Eucharist, we worship Jesus, who is more sublime than our eyes can see or our minds comprehend. We bow down and worship Him in faith.

The Magi find Mary and the Child *in a house* (Matthew 2:11), which does not contradict the account of Luke, who indicates that Jesus was born in a *manger* (Luke 2:7). In the first century, some homes had a place for animals on one level and family living quarters above, or behind. The duration of time between the birth of Jesus and the arrival of the Magi, may also have afforded enough time for Joseph to find more suitable accommodations for the Holy Family.

Dreams, dreams, and more dreams—Dreams play a prominent role in the Bible, and especially in these early chapters of Matthew's Gospel. First, an angel of the Lord appears to Joseph in a dream, charging him to take Mary as his wife, despite his reservations, and name the child Jesus (Matthew 1:20ff). Next, the wise men are warned in a dream not to return to Herod, but to depart for their country by a different route (Matthew 2:12). Then, an angel of the Lord appears to Joseph in another dream and tells him to flee with the Child and Mary to Egypt (Matthew 2:13ff).

Jewish readers of old and Christian readers today recall Old Testament Joseph, with his coat of many colors, or *long robe with sleeves* (Genesis 37:3), who dreamed dreams and interpreted dreams. Joseph, sold into slavery in Egypt, later saved his family from starvation, by bringing them to safety in Egypt with him (Genesis 37–50). Egypt often provided a place of refuge for the Jews (Genesis 46:3–4; Jeremiah 26:21; 42:13ff). Now, the New Testament Joseph, prompted by an angel in a dream, takes Mary and Jesus to safety in Egypt, escaping from the murderous rage of Herod, and fulfilling the words of another Old Testament prophet: *out of Egypt I called my son* (Hosea 11:1).

Slaughter of the innocents—In the Old Testament, Pharaoh ordered midwives to drown the Hebrew baby boys (Exodus 1:15–16). Now Herod, who had murdered his wife, mother-in-law, and some sons who he thought were trying to usurp his power, orders the slaughter of innocent Hebrew baby boys. These parallel passages depict Jesus as a new Moses. As Pharaoh's daughter rescued baby Moses from certain death (Exodus 2), so the angel and Joseph rescue baby Jesus from impending death. According to census estimates for that time, probably about twenty baby boys were killed in Bethlehem. The Catholic Church celebrates the feast of the Holy Innocents on December 28th. Though they are too young to speak, these children bear witness to Christ and die for Him, though they do not know it. How happy would their parents be to be re-united with them in heaven!

Herod was tricked and flew into a furious rage. He would do anything, including murder innocent people to protect his interests and his power. Herod's atrocities are well documented by the historian Josephus. Sadly, his successors followed in his evil footsteps. Herod's legacy is one of paranoia, lust for power, and murder.

Presently, a slaughter of the innocents continues in our society, in which people will do anything, including take the life of an innocent unborn child, if a pregnancy gets in the way of someone's convenience or plans. Millions of innocents are aborted every year. And millions of women and men later mourn the decisions they made in haste, sometimes under pressure from others. Jesus was inconvenient to Herod. Today, innocent, unborn children are often seen as an inconvenience. But, increasingly, helping hands reach out to give pregnant women and abortion-vulnerable babies a safe haven and a chance to spare the life of the unborn child.

"A voice was heard in Ramah, wailing and loud lamentation, Rachel weeping for her children; she refused to be consoled, because they were no more" (Matthew 2:18). Hear the echo in this verse from an earlier verse in Jeremiah. *Thus says the Lord: "A voice is heard in Ramah, lamentation and bitter weeping. Rachel is weeping for her children; she refuses to be comforted for her children, because they are not"* (Jeremiah 31:15). This verse offers consolation to post-abortive women and men in Rachel's Vineyard and Project Rachel retreats and ministries. The Catholic Church strives to save the life of the unborn child, and also offers healing to those who suffer the consequences often experienced after abortion.

Thus says the Lord: *"A voice is heard in Ramah,* *lamentation and bitter weeping.* *Rachel is weeping for her children;* *she refuses to be comforted for her children,* *because they are not"* (Jeremiah 31:15).	*"A voice was heard in Ramah,* *wailing and loud lamentation,* *Rachel weeping for her children;* *she refused to be consoled,* *because they were no more"* (Matthew 2:18).

A mother's loss of a child causes a singular and profound grief. Any parent who loses a child experiences unimaginable grief and sorrow. God the Father also suffered the loss of a Child who was unwanted, unloved by many, and ultimately killed. God is well acquainted with grief. Anyone can go to God the Father with his or her shame and sorrows. God understands. He can forgive and heal.

Return from Egypt to Nazareth—After Herod's death, an angel of the Lord appears once again in a dream to Joseph, saying, *"Rise, take the child and his mother, and go to the land of Israel, for those who sought the child's life are dead"* (Matthew 2:20). Similarly, after Moses had fled into the land of Midian, the Lord called him to return to the people of Israel, *"for the men who were seeking your life are dead"* (Exodus 4:19). Jesus emerges, once again, as a new Moses.

Joseph, Mary, and Jesus return to the land of Israel after the death of Herod the Great. However, Herod's son Archelaus now rules over Judea, Samaria, and Idumea. Sadly, the apple does not fall far from the tree. Archelaus continues exercising such horrible brutality that he is eventually exiled. But, Joseph, once again warned of this situation in a dream, takes Mary and Jesus and moves the Holy Family into the obscure village of Nazareth in Galilee. Since Joseph was a carpenter, there would be ample opportunities for work in the nearby city of Sepphoris, which Herod Antipas was rebuilding as his capital at that time.

Matthew reports: *And he went and dwelt in a city called Nazareth, that what was spoken by the prophets might be fulfilled, "He shall be called a Nazarene"* (Matthew 2:23). Unfortunately, not everything spoken by the prophets was written. No written Old Testament prophecy with this wording can be identified. In Hebrew, the word *netser* means "branch." The Old Testament prophecies may present a play-on-words, representing a common image, recognizable to the Jewish people of that time. Isaiah prophecies: *There shall come forth a <u>shoot</u> from the stump of Jesse, and <u>a branch</u> shall grow out of his roots. And the Spirit of the Lord shall rest upon him . . ."* (Isaiah 11:1–2). David was the son of Jesse, and Jesus falls in the line of David, so Jesus is a branch on the Jesse tree.

Jeremiah prophecies: *"Behold, the days are coming, says the* Lord, *when I will raise up for David <u>a righteous Branch</u>, and he shall reign as king and deal wisely, and shall execute justice and righteousness in the land. In his days Judah will be saved, and Israel will dwell securely. And this is the name by which he will be called: 'The* Lord *is our righteousness'"* (Jeremiah 23:5–6). Jesus is our righteous branch.

Zechariah speaks the word of the Lord, as follows, *'Thus says the* Lord *of hosts, "Behold, the man whose name is the <u>Branch</u>: for he shall grow up in his place, and he shall build the temple of the* Lord. *It is he who shall build the temple of the* Lord, *and shall bear royal honor, and shall sit and rule upon his throne"* (Zechariah 6:12–13a). While these verses may seem oblique today, they may have resonated with a familiarity to Jewish readers in the time of Matthew, in such a way that they recognized Jesus of Nazareth as the promised Messiah of Israel.

What are we to bring You?

Each creature, the work of your hands, offers you a sign of gratitude: the angels, their hymn; the heavens, the star; the Magi, their gifts; the shepherds, their adoration . . . and all mankind, we offer you a virgin mother.

Mary is the gift of mankind to Christ. And this in turn means that the Lord does not want some *thing* from man, but man himself. He wants our heart; indeed, he wants our whole being. He wants our faith and the life that is based on faith. And from this life, he wants those gifts of which he will speak at the Last Judgment: food and clothing for the poor, compassion and mutual love, a word that gives consolation, and a presence that brings comfort to the persecuted, the imprisoned, the abandoned, the lost.

What can we offer you, O Christ? We certainly offer him too little if all we do is to exchange costly presents with one another, gifts that are not the expression of our own selves and of a gratitude that otherwise remains silent. Let us try to offer him our faith and our own selves, even if only in the form of the prayer: "I believe, Lord, help my unbelief!" And . . . let us not forget the many in whom he suffers on earth.

The Christmas icon of the Eastern Churches . . . shows the profound connection between Christmas and Easter, the crib and the cross. . . . Saint Joseph is given a very strange function in this icon. He sits to the side, deep in thought. The tempter stands before him, in the garments of a shepherd, and says: "An old man like you cannot beget children or a virgin give birth any more than this staff can burst into flower." . . . A storm of contradictory thoughts raged in Joseph's heart, and he was perplexed; but enlightened by the Holy Spirit, he sang: "Alleluia!" . . . Saint Joseph portrays a constantly recurring drama—our own drama.

Again and again, the tempter tells us that only the visible world exists. There is no Incarnation of God, and the Virgin does not give birth. These affirmations deny that God knows us, that he loves us, and that he is capable of acting in this world. On the deepest level, therefore, this is a denial of the glory of God. And this is the typical temptation of our own age . . .

Let us ask God in his kindness to send the light of the Holy Spirit to our hearts, too. And let us ask him to permit us to leave behind the rigidity of our intellectual reflections, so that we may see the light with great joy and may sing: "Alleluia! Christ is truly born; Christ has become man. . . . We offer you a virgin mother." We bring you our own selves, something more valuable than any gift of money; we bring the wealth of the true faith to you, the God and Savior of our souls.

Pope Benedict XVI, *The Blessing of Christmas,*
(San Francisco: Ignatius Press, 2007), 112–116

1. What prophecy comes to fulfillment in these verses?

Micah 5:2
Matthew 2:1–5
Luke 2:4

2. Explain these prophecies and promises.

Jeremiah 23:5–6
Matthew 2:2
CCC 439

3. What did Herod tell the Wise Men? Matthew 2:7–8

4. Where was Jesus found by shepherds and by Wise Men?

Shepherds	Luke 2:15–16	
Wise Men	Matthew 2:10–11	

5. What significance can you find in Jesus' place of birth? CCC 525

6. What did the Wise Men do when they saw Jesus and Mary? Matthew 2:11

7. What gifts did the Wise Men give Jesus? Tobit 13:11; Matthew 2:11

8. Who else offered similar gifts? To whom were they offered? For what purpose?

1 Kings 10:10		
Matthew 26:7		
John 19:39		

9. What does the Epiphany (feast of the Magi) reveal? CCC 528

10. Why did the Wise Men change their return itinerary? Matthew 2:12

* When do Catholics observe Epiphany? How do you celebrate Epiphany?

11. Describe the drama in Matthew 2:13.

12. How does Joseph respond? Matthew 2:14

13. Find a fulfillment of prophecy.

Hosea 11:1
Matthew 2:14–15

14. How does Herod respond to being deceived? Matthew 2:16

15. When was a similar slaughter proposed? Exodus 1:15–16

16. Who was saved from this slaughter? How? Exodus 2:1–10

* What do the flight into Egypt and massacre of the innocents show? CCC 530

* What practical efforts attempt to thwart the massacre of innocents today?

** What could you do to protect innocent, vulnerable, unborn children?

17. How many times do angels appear to Joseph in dreams? Matthew 1:20–2:20

18. Compare the following verses.

Exodus 4:19
Matthew 2:20

19. Where did Joseph settle the Holy Family? Matthew 2:21–23

20. What do gold, frankincense, and myrrh symbolize? Matthew 2:11

*** How important is gift giving at Christmas? Where did the idea originate?

Monthly Social Activity

This month, your small group will meet for coffee, tea, or a simple breakfast, lunch, or dessert in someone's home. Pray for this social event, and for your host or hostess. Try, if at all possible, to attend.

The Magi brought gifts of gold, frankincense and myrrh to Jesus in Bethlehem (Matthew 2:1–12). Think of a gift that you gave to another person that was greatly appreciated.

Some examples:

❋ *I made a project in school that I gave to my mother.*

❋ *Anonymously, I gave some money to a family in need.*

❋ *I gave the gift of time to an elderly relative in a nursing home.*

CHAPTER 3

Baptism in the Jordan
Matthew 3

I baptize you with water for repentance,
but he who is coming after me is mightier than I,
whose sandals I am not worthy to carry;
he will baptize you with the Holy Spirit and with fire.
Matthew 3:11

The Preaching of John the Baptist—Matthew leaps ahead thirty years, from the infancy of Jesus to His adult life and the commencement of His public ministry. Jesus moves from Nazareth in Galilee to the wilderness of Judea at the Jordan River, probably near the mouth of the Dead Sea, where John the Baptist preaches an urgent message of repentance, fulfilling the prophecy of Isaiah, *the voice in the wilderness, preparing the way of the Lord* (Isaiah 40:3; Matthew 3:3).

The Jordan River places prominently, geographically and historically, for the nation of Israel. God worked great miracles at the Jordan River, which the Jewish people still recall and cherish.

- ✦ Joshua led the Chosen People across the Jordan River into the Promised Land (Joshua 3:14–17).
- ✦ Elijah the prophet was taken up into heaven, in a whirlwind, on a fiery chariot, at the Jordan River (2 Kings 2:1–12).
- ✦ Elisha directed Naaman, the Syrian leper to wash in the Jordan River, where he was healed of his leprosy (2 Kings 5:1–14).

John the Baptist's central message at the Jordan River is: *"Repent, for the kingdom of heaven is at hand* (Matthew 3:2), proclaiming for the first time, the main theme of Matthew's Gospel. Jesus later affirms and re-states John's teaching in the desert, sometimes repeating John's words verbatim.

John the Baptist's Words	Jesus' Words
"Repent, for the kingdom of heaven is at hand" (Matthew 3:2).	*"Repent, for the kingdom of heaven is at hand"* (Matthew 4:17).
"You brood of vipers! Who warned you to flee from the wrath to come?" (Matthew 3:7).	*"You brood of vipers, how are you to escape being sentenced to hell?"* (Matthew 23:33).
"Every tree therefore that does not bear good fruit is cut down and thrown into the fire." (Matthew 3:10).	*"Every tree that does not bear good fruit is cut down and thrown into the fire."* (Matthew 7:19).

A Levite, John the Baptist, son of Zechariah the priest and Elizabeth, kinswoman of the Virgin Mary (Luke 1) introduces the public ministry of his relative Jesus. John the Baptist's clothing: *a garment of camel's hair, and a leather belt around his waist* (Matthew 3:4) reveals him as the new Elijah: *"He wore a garment of haircloth, with a belt of leather about his loins"* (2 Kings 1:8). Jesus later declares that John *is* Elijah: *For all the prophets and the law prophesied until John; and if you are willing to accept it, he is Elijah who is to come* (Matthew 11:13–14). John's diet, comprised of locusts and wild honey, reflects the ritually clean foods available to desert dwellers. Jews were permitted to eat locusts (Leviticus 11:22). This later becomes the diet of Christian monks living in the desert.

Since John the Baptist was born to elderly parents, he may have been orphaned at a young age. If so, he may have been raised by the monastic, Essene community in Qumran near the Dead Sea. The Essenes, a priestly group, seriously preparing for the coming of the Messiah, opposed the Sadducees, a religious, political group of Zadokite priestly background, in charge of the Jerusalem Temple. The Pharisees were a religious group demanding rigorous adherence to the regulations of the Torah and oral traditions concerning ritual purity, tithing, and sabbath observance. Pharisees were rigid and demanding.

A charismatic leader, John the Baptist draws followers from Jerusalem and all Judea to the wilderness region around the Jordan River. John baptizes people in a religious rite of cleansing following their repentance, analogous to Old Testament priestly ritual washings. John calls the Pharisees and Sadducees, coming to him for baptism, a brood of vipers, because they are deceitful and corrupt leaders, who are dangerously rigid and exclusive. Clinging to ethnic identity, they believe that as sons of Abraham, they are saved and blessed. But, salvation is not hereditary. Each person is judged alone.

John announces the coming of the Greater One. *"I baptize you with water for repentance, but he who is coming after me is mightier than I, whose sandals I am not worthy to carry; he will baptize you with the Holy Spirit and with fire. His winnowing fork is in his hand, and he will clear his threshing floor and gather his wheat into the granary, but the chaff he will burn with unquenchable fire"* (Matthew 3:11–12). Jeremiah used the winnowing fork to foretell God's judgment of exile on Judah: *"I have winnowed them with a winnowing fork in the gates of the land; I have bereaved them, I have destroyed my people; they did not turn from their ways"* (Jeremiah 15:7). Disciples of rabbis performed many servile tasks, except removing sandals. Humbly, John shows his submissiveness to Jesus.

The Baptism of Jesus in the Jordan—Saint John Paul II highlighted this event in the life of Jesus, by making it the first mystery for meditation in the Luminous Mysteries of the Rosary. As Jesus approaches, John is confused. Jesus, without sin, does not need repentance or baptism. John does not understand, but obeys. In accepting this ritual cleansing, Jesus identifies with sinful humanity, and submits Himself entirely to the Father's will. Out of love, Jesus, the Suffering Servant, accepts a baptism of death for the remission of the sins of the world (CCC 536).

When Jesus was baptized, he went up immediately from the water, and behold, the heavens were opened and he saw the Spirit of God descending like a dove, and alighting on him; and behold, a voice from heaven, saying, "This is my beloved Son, with whom I am well pleased" (Matthew 3:16–17). This passage becomes the first New Testament revelation of the Holy Trinity—God the Father, Jesus the Son, and the Holy Spirit appear together. Artists beautifully depict this scene at the Jordan River, attempting to illustrate the mystery of the Blessed Trinity, which we can never comprehend.

The Spirit of God descending like a dove, recalls *the Spirit of God was moving over the face of the waters* (Genesis 1:2) at the creation of the world. The appearance like a dove is also reminiscent of the dove that Noah sent out from the ark after the flood (Genesis 8:8–12), which did not return, as the earth became habitable again. The Genesis references allude to a new creation—the beginning of a new kingdom of God, which Jesus is establishing for humanity.

The voice from heaven is the voice of God the Father, revealing that Jesus is the divine Son of God. *Out of heaven he let you hear his voice* (Deuteronomy 4:36). God the Father witnesses to the identity of Jesus of Nazareth. There are flashbacks to Old Testament imagery in this scene. Jesus, the new Isaac, fulfills the prophecy. Jesus, the Suffering Servant, will offer the perfect sacrifice that was pre-figured by Isaac. Jesus will carry the wood of the Cross and sins of humanity.

+ God commanded Abraham: *"Take your son, your only-begotten son Isaac, whom you love, and go to the land of Moriah, and offer him there as a burnt offering* (Genesis 22:2).
+ The Psalmist proclaims: *I will tell of the decree of the LORD; He said to me, "You are my son, today I have begotten you"* (Psalm 2:7).
+ Isaiah prophesied of a Suffering Servant: *Behold my servant, whom I uphold, my chosen, in whom my soul delights; I have put my Spirit upon him, he will bring forth justice to the nations* (Isaiah 42:1).

Many, my beloved, are the true witnesses to Christ. The Father bears witness from heaven to His Son. The Holy Spirit bears witness, coming down bodily in the form of a dove. The Archangel Gabriel bears witness, bringing good tidings to Mary. The Virgin Mother of God bears witness . . .

And if your piety is unfeigned the Holy Spirit will come down upon you also, and from on high a paternal voice will sound over you: not, "This is My Son," but "This is now become My son." The "is" belongs to Him alone, because "In the beginning was the Word, and the Word was with God, and the Word was God." To Him belongs the "is," because always the Son of God He is. To you belongs the "is now become," because you have sonship not by nature, but have received it by adoption.

Saint Cyril of Jerusalem (AD 315–386), *Catechetical Lectures*, 10,19; 3,14

29

Catholics profess belief in the Blessed Trinity, even though the Trinity is a mystery, beyond human comprehension. Sacred Scripture provides enough evidence for a reasonable person to trust and believe. God the Father and the Holy Spirit are pure spirit, without bodies. Yet, in order to visualize them in our mind's eye, we try to imagine them in ways that are comprehensible to mere mortals, and revere them in the Sign of the Cross.

The Lord Jesus Himself has not only, as God, given the Holy Spirit, but also, as Man, He has received Him. That is why He is said to be "full of grace and of the Holy Spirit." And it is written more plainly of Him in the Acts of the Apostles, "because God anointed Him with the Holy Spirit." He was not anointed as if with a visible oil, but with the gift of grace, which is signified by the visible anointing with which the Church anoints the baptized. Neither was Christ anointed by the Holy Spirit when, at His baptism, the Holy Spirit descended upon Him as a dove; for in this He deigned to prefigure His Body, that is, His Church, in which the baptized receive the Holy Spirit in a special way.

But it is to be understood that He was anointed in that mystical and invisible anointing when the Word of God was made flesh, that is, when a human nature, without any preceding merits of good works, was joined to the Divine Word in the womb of the Virgin, in such a way as to become one person with the Divine Word. That is why we confess that He was born of the Holy Spirit and the Virgin Mary; for it were very foolish of us to believe that He received the Holy Spirit when He was already thirty years of age.

Saint Augustine of Hippo (AD 354–430), *The Trinity*, 15, 26, 46

Jesus, although sinless, identified with our sinful, human condition. He had no need for any type of repentance or baptism. But, Jesus completely identified with us, and in perfect submission embraced the will of the Father. Saint Peter proclaims: *He [Jesus] committed no sin; no guile was found on his lips. When he was reviled, he did not revile in return; when he suffered, he did not threaten; but he trusted to him who judges justly. He himself bore our sins in his body on the tree, that we might die to sin and live to righteousness* (1 Peter 2:22–24).

Jesus, the perfect, sinless One, chose to identify with us, sinners. He submitted to water baptism by John, to reveal the Blessed Trinity. Joshua brought the Chosen People through the Jordan River to the Promised Land. Jesus, the new Joshua, will lead His people through the waters of baptism into His kingdom. If we are buried with Him in baptism, we hope to rise with Him in the resurrection of the body, at the end of the age, and enter into His everlasting kingdom, where *"he will wipe away every tear from their eyes, and death shall be no more, neither shall there be mourning nor crying nor pain any more"* (Revelation 21:4).

1. What is John the Baptist's message? Matthew 3:2

2. Define "repentance" or "contrition." CCC 1451

3. Who does John resemble? 2 Kings 1:8

4. What is significant about John the Baptist's diet? Leviticus 11:22; Matthew 3:4

5. Who is John the Baptist? CCC 523

6. How do John and Jesus feel about the Pharisees and Sadducees?

Matthew 3:7
Matthew 23:33
Matthew 3:8–10
Matthew 7:19

* Can you identify a modern-day prophet?

7. How does John explain his baptism and introduce Jesus? Matthew 3:11

8. Where does Jesus come from? Matthew 3:13

9. How does John the Baptist respond to Jesus' request for baptism? Matthew 3:14

10. Why does Jesus, although sinless, request baptism?

Matthew 3:15
1 Peter 2:22–24
CCC 536

11. What does Jesus' action demonstrate? CCC 1224

** Describe a humble and submissive person you know.

12. How does a person today emulate Jesus? CCC 537

13. When and how does Jesus' public ministry begin? CCC 535

14. What happened when Jesus was baptized in the Jordan? Matthew 3:16–17

15. What does a dove represent in the Bible? CCC 701

16. When was a dove significant in the Old Testament? Genesis 8:8–12

17. Identify the Three Persons of the Blessed Trinity found in Matthew 3:16–17.

18. What significant events foretell the Messiah in the passages?

Isaiah 11:2
Isaiah 61:1
CCC 1286

19. Identify persons of the Blessed Trinity in these passages.

Matthew 17:1–8
CCC 253

20. What is the importance of the Most Holy Trinity?

CCC 234
CCC 237
CCC 249

* Which Divine Person of the Blessed Trinity is most elusive to you?

** How can you respond to someone who says, "The Trinity is not in the Bible"?

CHAPTER 4

Calling Disciples
Matthew 4

From that time
Jesus began to preach, saying,
"Repent, for the kingdom of heaven is at hand."
Matthew 4:17

Temptation of Jesus—Just after the amazing manifestation of the Blessed Trinity at the Baptism of the Lord, the Spirit leads Jesus into the wilderness to experience temptation by the devil, the fate of all humanity. Jesus shares in our humanity, with all of its weaknesses and challenges, and yet He masters and overcomes all of the temptations thrown at Him, without ever falling into sin.

> Temptation—solicitation to sin, whether by persuasion or offering some pleasure. It arises from the world, the flesh, or the devil.
> + Temptation from the *world* is the attractiveness of bad example and the psychological pressure to conform.
> + Temptations from the *flesh* are all the urges of concupiscence, whether carnal or spiritual, where man's fallen nature has built-in tendencies to the seven capital sins *[pride, avarice, lust, envy, gluttony, anger, and sloth]*.
> + Demonic *[the devil]* temptations arise from instigations of the evil spirit, whose method is to encourage every form of avarice or selfishness, in order to lead one to pride, and through pride to all other sins.
> Hardon, John A., S.J., *Pocket Catholic Dictionary*,
> (New York: Doubleday, 1985), 428–429

Matthew reveals a critical spiritual truth—the devil is real, seductive, and powerful. Jesus knows the devil is a liar, a murderer from the beginning, and has nothing to do with the truth (John 8:44). The evil one has no creative abilities, which belong to God alone. All Satan can do is distort the good things of God and promise delights, which will not bring true joy. What the tempter promises as desirable and pleasurable, soon turns deadly and sour. The evil spirit dangles pleasure, power, and success in front of the eyes. But, apart from the perfect will of God the Father, those things which appear good, often bring alienation from God and loved ones, and ultimately result in pain, shame, and sorrow.

Jesus is more powerful than the evil spirit. Even in hunger after fasting, He will not be distracted from the Father's plan and the perfect purpose for His life. Jesus has all power, but does not use it apart from the Father's will. Jesus has developed the strength of character and will to resist the devil's temptations.

The Spirit's command leads Him into the desert *"to be tempted by the devil"* (Matthew 4:1). This action is prefaced by interior recollection, and this recollection is also, inevitably, an inner struggle for fidelity to the task, a struggle against all the distortions of the task that claim to be its true fulfillment. It is a descent into the perils besetting mankind, for there is no other way to lift up fallen humanity. Jesus has to enter into the drama of human existence, for that belongs to the core of His mission; He has to penetrate it completely, down to its uttermost depths, in order to find the "lost sheep," to bear it on His shoulders, and to bring it home.

The Apostle's Creed speaks of Jesus' descent "into hell." This descent not only took place in and after His death, but accompanies Him along his entire journey. He must recapitulate the whole of history from its beginnings—from Adam on; He must go through, suffer through, the whole of it, in order to transform it. . . . We will see Jesus wrestling once again with His mission during his agony on the Mount of Olives. But the "temptations" are with Him every step of the way. . .

At the heart of all temptations is the act of pushing God aside because we perceive him as secondary, if not actually superfluous and annoying, in comparison with all the apparently far more urgent matters that fill our lives. Constructing a world by our own lights, without reference to God, building on our own foundation; refusing to acknowledge the reality of anything beyond the political and material, while setting God aside as an illusion—that is the temptation that threatens us. . .

God is the issue: Is he real, reality itself, or isn't he? Is he good, or do we have to invent the good ourselves? The God question is the fundamental question, and it sets us right down at the crossroads of human existence. What must the Savior of the world do or not do? That is the question the temptations of Jesus are about. . .

The devil cites Holy Scripture in order to lure Jesus into his trap. . . . The devil proves to be a Bible expert who can quote the Psalm exactly. The whole conversation takes the form of a dispute between two Bible scholars. . . . The theological debate between Jesus and the devil is a dispute over the correct interpretation of Scripture, and it is relevant to every period of history. . . . We are dealing here with the vast question as to how we can and cannot know God, how we are related to God and how we can lose him. The arrogance that would make God an object and impose our laboratory conditions upon him is incapable of finding him. For it already implies that we deny God as God by placing ourselves above him, by discarding the dimension of love. . .

[Jesus] did not leap into the abyss. He did not tempt God. But He did descend into the abyss of death, into the night of abandonment, and into the desolation of the defenseless. He ventured *this* leap as an act of God's love for men. He knew that, ultimately, when He leaped He could only fall into the kindly hands of the Father.

Pope Benedict XVI, *Jesus of Nazareth,*
(New York: Doubleday, 2007), 26–38

Temptation is not synonymous with sin. Everyone experiences temptations, but only in entertaining or succumbing to these temptations does one actually commit sin. And in the event of sin, the Sacrament of Reconciliation enables one to experience the love, compassion, and forgiveness of God—to get back on track. God's mercy prods the sinner to return to the state of grace.

Saint Paul warns believers concerning temptations from the world. *Do not be conformed to this world but be transformed by the renewal of your mind, that you may prove what is the will of God, what is good and acceptable and perfect* (Romans 12:2). Paul also encourages believers to walk by the Spirit, not gratifying the desires of the flesh. *We all once lived in the passions of our flesh, following the desires of body and mind, and so we were by nature children of wrath, like the rest of mankind* (Ephesians 2:3). Mastery over the flesh brings true freedom.

Saint John exhorts believers: *All that is in the world, the lust of the flesh and the lust of the eyes and the pride of life, is not of the Father but is of the world And the world passes away, and the lust of it; but he who does the will of God abides forever* (1 John 2:16–17). Prayer and receiving the sacraments enable one to stay in God's will.

Saint Peter alerts believers concerning the devil. *Be sober, be watchful. Your adversary the devil prowls around like a roaring lion, seeking some one to devour. Resist him, firm in your faith, knowing that the same experience of suffering is required of your brotherhood throughout the world* (1 Peter 5:8–9). Jesus gives a perfect example of how to deal with the world, the flesh, and the devil.

The apostles provide excellent, practical advice for believers. With God's grace and help, the world, the flesh, and the devil can be overcome. Discipline enables one to master his or her passions and to do battle with evil influences in the world. The earlier in life that one can develop self-discipline and self-mastery, the better off he or she will be. No temptation becomes too great to face with God's help. Forewarned is forearmed. Be humble and diligent, lest you fall. *No temptation has overtaken you that is not common to man. God is faithful, and he will not let you be tempted beyond your strength, but with the temptation will also provide the way of escape, that you may be able to endure it* (1 Corinthians 10:13).

The kingdom of heaven is at hand. Jesus begins His ministry in Galilee with the same words as those of John the Baptist. *"Repent for the kingdom of heaven is at hand"* (Matthew 3:2; 4:17). Repentance involves changing direction. To repent means to turn away from sin and selfishness, and to submit in humility to the will of God. Repentance requires sorrow for sin, and firm resolve to grow in virtue. For most believers, repentance begins with conversion and continues throughout life.

The "kingdom of heaven" emerges as the major theme of Matthew's Gospel. This term is used synonymously with the term "kingdom of God." Matthew writes primarily with Jewish readers in mind. Jews of the first century and many Jews today have profound respect for the "Divine Name" and do not pronounce it or write it casually. You may have read a contemporary letter to the editor of a major newspaper, written by a Jewish person, who refers to the Almighty as "G–d" out of respect and reluctance to write the Divine Name. Matthew uses this reverent circumlocution, "kingdom of heaven" more than thirty times in his Gospel. But on at least four occasions, Matthew also reverts to the explicit term "kingdom of God" (Matthew 12:28; 19:24; 21:31, 43).

The Old Testament prophet Daniel reported a vision of the Messiah. *I saw in the night visions, and behold, with the clouds of heaven there came one like a son of man, and he came to the Ancient of Days and was presented before him. And to him was given dominion and glory and kingdom, that all peoples, nations, and languages should serve him; his dominion is an everlasting dominion, which shall not pass away, and his kingdom one that shall not be destroyed* (Daniel 7:13–14). Isaiah, the prophet, foretold the righteous reign of the coming King. *In the latter time he will make glorious the way of the sea, the land beyond the Jordan, Galilee of the nations. The people who walked in darkness have seen a great light; those who dwelt in a land of deep darkness, on them has light shined* (Isaiah 9:1–2).

Jesus fulfills the Old Testament visions and prophecies. The Son of man comes into the darkness of sinful, lost humanity to establish His kingdom of light and truth, which will last forever. God establishes the kingdom of heaven in and through His Son Jesus. In essence, where Jesus is, there is the kingdom. Jesus brings the kingdom of heaven in the power of His words and miracles.

Entering the kingdom of God requires an individual's humble, human response, to God's grace and invitation. The theme song in hell is probably: "I did it MY way." The theme song for entrance into the kingdom of heaven may be found in Matthew: *"Thy will be done"* (Matthew 4:19). The believer gives up preconceived notions and follows Jesus to learn the ways of God and the will of the Father.

While Jesus comes to earth to establish the kingdom of God, there remains an eschatological dimension of the kingdom that will not unfold until Jesus returns in glory at the end of the age. Jesus first comes as a Suffering Servant. But, Jesus will come again to judge the living and the dead. At that time, Jesus will come in glory with full splendor and the magnificence of His kingdom will unfold. *"Then will appear the sign of the Son of man in heaven, and then all the tribes of the earth will mourn, and they will see the Son of man coming on the clouds of heaven with power and great glory; and he will send out his angels with a loud trumpet call, and they will gather his elect from the four winds, from one end of heaven to the other"* (Matthew 24:30–31). Jesus establishes His kingdom on earth in His Church (Matthew 16:18–19; 18:18–20) and appoints a shepherd, Peter. So, to enter the kingdom of heaven, repent, believe, and follow Jesus. Remain in His Catholic Church under the shepherds He appoints, the pope and bishops in union with him.

Jesus calls Disciples—In the Holy Land in the first century, prospective students traditionally sought out a rabbi to be a mentor and teacher. Often, a father might seek out a rabbi to tutor his son. Even today, parents seek out a school or a teacher to instruct a child in music or art, or a coach for sports. But, Jesus once again turns things upside down. Jesus takes the initiative. He seeks out those who will become His disciples. Luke's Gospel reveals that Jesus often withdrew for prayer, and sometimes spent the entire night in prayer to discern the will of the Father. So, Jesus calls disciples in accord to the Father's perfect plan.

God calls people according to the particular plan He has for their lives. God called Abraham out of his land to be the father of a great nation (Genesis 12). Jacob (Israel) was called by God to father twelve sons, the twelve tribes of Israel (Genesis 49). God called Moses, revealed the Divine Name, and brought the Chosen People out of slavery in Egypt (Exodus 1–14). God brought prophets out from their farms or vineyards. Jesus exercises the divine imperative in calling apostles.

The Sea of Galilee, an exceedingly deep and often violent body of water, provides a rich source of food for the people. The lake is about thirteen miles long and seven miles at its widest point. Simon and Andrew, James and John were professional fisherman, whose fathers and grandfathers before them were probably fishermen as well. They were most likely prosperous, due to hot, backbreaking work that sometimes yielded a good haul, but sometimes yielded nothing at all.

As he [Jesus] walked by the Sea of Galilee, he saw two brothers, Simon who is called Peter and Andrew his brother, casting a net into the sea; for they were fishermen. And he said to them, "Follow me, and I will make you fishers of men." Immediately they left their nets and followed him (Matthew 4:18–20). Peter and Andrew respond without hesitation. They may have heard Jesus preaching in the area. The response of James and John, sons of Zebedee, is also immediate, as they leave their father and their livelihood. Peter, James, and John will become the most intimate of Jesus' apostles, witnessing the Transfiguration, the raising of Jairus' daughter from death, and Jesus' agony in Gethsemane (Mark 14:33).

The same immediate response has occurred many times over the centuries, as individuals leave everything to follow Jesus. While God doesn't call every person to leave behind father, mother, and livelihood, He does call everyone to follow Him closely. Sometimes people hear a call from God in childhood. Some respond immediately to their call from God, others reflect, pray, wait, and consider. The fact that you are studying God's Word in a serious way reveals that God has showered His grace and mercy upon you and you are answering His call.

God may be calling you for a particular work in His kingdom. He has given you gifts and talents that you can make available to Him for the building up of His body. God invites us to do spiritual and corporal works of mercy, in our families and communities. Listen carefully to the voice of God. When God calls you and invites you to follow Him into some work or ministry, respond immediately and joyfully. God blesses obedience in ways beyond what we can ask or imagine.

What is the Kingdom of Heaven?

What is the Kingdom of Heaven? Jesus did not go out of His way to explain it. He pronounced it from the very start of his Gospel: "The Kingdom of Heaven is at hand"—even today it is nearby, among us—however He never lets us see it directly, but always by reflection. . . . He prefers to leave it open to interpretation, with parables and similes, manifesting above all the effects: the Kingdom of Heaven can change the world, like yeast hidden in dough; it is small and humble like a mustard seed, which however will become tall like a tree. Two parables on which we reflect help us understand that the Kingdom of God is present in the very person of Jesus. He is the hidden treasure; He is the pearl of great value. One understands the joy of the farmer and merchant: they had found Him! It is the joy we each have when we discover the closeness and the presence of Jesus in our life—a presence which transforms our existence and makes us open to the needs of our brothers and sisters.

You may ask me: *How does one find the Kingdom of God?* Each of us has a particular journey; each of us has a path in life. For some the encounter with Jesus is awaited, desired, long sought, as it is revealed to us in the parable of the merchant who travels the world in search of something valuable. For others it happens suddenly, almost by chance, as in the parable of the farmer. This reminds us that God allows Himself to be met, because He is the first who desires to encounter us, and the first to seek that encounter with us. He came to be "God with us." And Jesus is among us. He is here today.

He said: "when you are gathered in my name, I am among you." The Lord is here. He is with us. He is in our midst! It is He who seeks us. It is He who lets Himself be found even by those who do not seek Him. At times He allows Himself to be found in unusual places and at unexpected times. When one finds Jesus, that person is captivated, overcome, and it is a joy to leave our usual lifestyle, sometimes desolate and apathetic, to embrace the Gospel, to let ourselves be guided by the new logic of love and of humble and unselfish service. . .

How does one obtain the Kingdom of God? Jesus is very explicit on this point: it's not enough to have enthusiasm, but the joy of discovery. It is essential to place the precious pearl of the Kingdom before every other, worldly good; we must place God first in our life, prefer Him to all else. Giving primacy to God means having the courage to say 'no' to evil, 'no' to violence, 'no' to oppression, to live a life in service of others and which fosters lawfulness and the common good. When a person discovers God, the true treasure, he abandons a selfish lifestyle and seeks to share with others the charity, which comes from God.

Pope Francis, *Homily,* July 26, 2014

1. Why did Jesus go into the wilderness?

Matthew 4:1
CCC 538

2. Who can you identify, and what can you learn from these passages?

Exodus 34:27–28
1 Kings 19:1–8
Matthew 4:2

3. What can you learn about the tempter?

John 8:44
CCC 395

4. Use a dictionary or the Catechism to define "temptation." CCC 2847

5. Explain the difference between temptation and "sin." CCC 1849, 1850, 1857

6. Compare these passages.

Matthew 4:3	Deuteronomy 8:3
Matthew 4:5–6	Matthew 4:7
Psalm 91:11–12	Deuteronomy 6:16
Matthew 4:8–9	Deuteronomy 6:13

7. What must people do? CCC 2135

8. What authority does Jesus exert? Matthew 4:10

9. How does Jesus win the battle with Satan? CCC 2849

10. How can you battle the evil one?

James 4:6–10
1 Peter 5:6–9

* List your most effective aids in times of temptation.

11. Explain the central theme of Matthew's Gospel.

Matthew 4:17
CCC 1720

12. What helps a person to repent? Matthew 4:17, CCC 1989

13. Who are the first two disciples called by Jesus? Matthew 4:18

14. What does Jesus say to Peter and Andrew? Matthew 4:19

15. How do Peter and Andrew respond to Jesus? Matthew 4:20

* Have you ever responded immediately to God's call?

** Have you ever hesitated in responding to a request for service?

16. Which pair of brothers does Jesus call next? Matthew 4:21

17. What response follows? Matthew 4:22

18. What three things does Jesus do in Galilee? Matthew 4:23

19. What was spread? Matthew 4:24

20. How did people respond to Jesus? Matthew 4:24–25

* How and when did you make an adult decision to follow Jesus?

Chapter 5

The Beatitudes
Matthew 5

*Blessed are those who are persecuted, for righteousness' sake,
for theirs is the kingdom of heaven.*
Matthew 5:10

Seeing the crowds, he went up on a mountain (Matthew 5:1), begins chapter five of Matthew. Matthew did not put the chapter marker here, however. At the beginning of the thirteenth century, Archbishop Stephen Langton of Canterbury (AD 1150–1228) divided the books of the Bible into chapters. Here, the Evangelist has just described the composition of the crowd in the last three verses of what is now chapter four. Those verses set the scene for the greatest homily of all time, the Sermon on the Mount, which spans chapters five, six, and seven of Matthew's Gospel.

Jesus' fame spread through the province of Syria (Matthew 4:24). Syrian pilgrims went to Jerusalem each year, following the great trade route through Galilee, passing by Capernaum. There, Matthew sat at his tax booth processing papers and inspecting goods. The crowds also included people not on pilgrimage—Galileans, Decapolitans, Transjordanians, and other Judeans (Matthew 4:25).

Just as Moses went up Mount Sinai to commune with God, receive the Law, and then instruct the people, from this elevated place, Jesus speaks with authority about *the kingdom of heaven*. Primarily addressing committed disciples, Jesus teaches them how to relate to God *your heavenly Father* (Matthew 5:16, 45, 48), Jesus Himself, who fulfills the law and the prophets (Matthew 5:17), one another, (Matthew 5:23ff), and enemies (Matthew 5:43ff). He gives a radical new teaching and a high standard of uprightness.

Let your light so shine before men, that they may see your good works and give glory to your Father who is in heaven (Matthew 5:16).	*Love your enemies and pray for those who persecute you, so that you may be sons of your Father who is in heaven* (Matthew 5:44–45).	*You, therefore, must be perfect, as your heavenly Father is perfect* (Matthew 5:48).

"Blessed are the poor in spirit, for theirs is the kingdom of heaven" (Matthew 5:3). Isaiah said of the Messiah: *with righteousness he shall judge the poor* (Isaiah 11:4). The *Anawim* (poor) held a special place of honor in the Old Testament, for from them would come the Messiah. Jesus could spot the poor in the crowd, by their shabby dress, sitting on the margins of the assembly, and Jesus drew them in. Generally, pilgrims had more wealth than the local people. These wealthy pilgrims were not offended to hear Jesus bless the poor, however, for they had come bringing the blessing of alms to distribute to the poor who dwelt in the land. When the rich make common cause with the poor, then they too become *poor in spirit*.

The kingdom of heaven highlights the first of the eight beatitudes, and also the last. In the previous chapters, Matthew summarizes the preaching of both John the Baptist and Jesus with these same words, *"Repent, for the kingdom of heaven is at hand"* (Matthew 3:2, 4:17). The Sermon on the Mount presents this teaching painted large. The phrase *kingdom of heaven* occurs four times in the opening section of the sermon (Matthew 5:3, 10, 19, 20). Jesus blesses the future citizens of His coming kingdom, though they may be despised at this time. Repentance is the starting point for believers.

"Blessed are those who mourn, for they shall be comforted" (Matthew 5:4). Another group easily noticed in the crowd were the mourners, because they wore black for a time after the loss of a loved one. Some of the rich wore black finery, while the poor wore black rags. The scourge of death cuts across social strata, to affect every family, rich or poor. Jesus Himself had mourned the death of his putative father, Saint Joseph, and He knew the keen pain of such a loss.

Families frequently choose the beatitudes for the funeral liturgy of a loved one. This second beatitude offers blessing to mourners, but all the beatitudes offer blessing to the deceased. Consider who is speaking. Jesus had come to earth for the express purpose of abolishing death. Only He can offer the ultimate comfort of eternal life. Those who mourn Jesus at His death: the women of Jerusalem, women who had accompanied Him from Galilee, and His distraught and confused apostles, including Matthew himself will be comforted by His Resurrection on Easter.

"Blessed are the meek, for they shall inherit the earth" (Matthew 5:5). If the poor lack money, the meek are powerless. Power, one of the great illusions of human life, prods people to climb for a lifetime to earn but a brief span at the top. Jesus chose to spend His life among the meek when He refused the devil's offer of an earthly kingdom; He would build a different kind of kingdom, based on a wholly different ethos. Jesus will change the world, and will use those who are meek to astound the proud. *The meek shall inherit the earth* is one of several phrases in the Sermon on the Mount that come from the wisdom literature of the Bible (Psalm 37).

"Blessed are those who hunger and thirst for righteousness, for they shall be satisfied" (Matthew 5:6). Hungry people on the fringes were probably begging for food. Matthew's form is longer than Luke's. Luke noted the poor, while Matthew has the *poor in spirit*; Luke reported the hungry, but Matthew notes those who *hunger after righteousness*. Undoubtedly, Jesus spoke about the beatitudes on many occasions during the course of His public ministry. Tailoring His remarks to the needs of each specific audience, He might have mentioned two beatitudes one day, four, six, or more on another. Therefore, the accounts in Luke and Matthew can both be correct, accurately transmitting what Jesus said on this day or on that.

Sermon on the Mount	Psalm 37
"Blessed are the poor in spirit, for theirs is the kingdom of heaven (Matthew 5:3).	*Better is a little that the righteous has than the abundance of many wicked* (Psalm 37:16).
Blessed are those who mourn, for they shall be comforted (Matthew 5:4).	*The wicked watches the righteous, and seeks to slay him. The LORD will not abandon him to his power* (Psalm 37:32–33).
Blessed are the meek, for they shall inherit the earth (Matthew 5:5).	*But the meek shall possess the land, and delight themselves in abundant prosperity* (Psalm 37:11).
Blessed are they who hunger and thirst for righteousness, for they shall be satisfied (Matthew 5:6).	*The LORD knows the days of the blameless, and their heritage will abide for ever; they are not put to shame in evil times, in the days of famine they have abundance* (Psalm 37:18–19).
Blessed are the merciful, for they shall obtain mercy (Matthew 5:7).	*He is ever giving liberally and lending, and his children become a blessing* (Psalm 37:26).
Blessed are the pure in heart, for they shall see God (Matthew 5:8).	*The law of his God is in his heart; his steps do not slip* (Psalm 37:31).
Blessed are the peacemakers, for they shall be called sons of God (Matthew 5:9).	*Mark the blameless man, and behold the upright, for there is posterity for the man of peace* (Psalm 37:37).
And in praying do not heap up empty phrases as the Gentiles do (Matthew 6:7).	*The mouth of the righteous utters wisdom, and his tongue speaks justice* (Psalm 37:30).
And lead us not into temptation, But deliver us from evil (Matthew 6:13).	*The LORD will not abandon him to his power, or let him be condemned when he is brought to trial* (Psalm 37:33).
God so clothes the grass of the field, which today is alive (Matthew 6:30).	*For they will soon fade like the grass* (Psalm 37:2).

"Blessed are the merciful, for they shall obtain mercy" (Matthew 5:7). Some of the people in the crowd help others in need, doing corporal works of mercy, and some doing spiritual works of mercy. Jesus honors those already putting into practice His gospel of mercy, along with those who later would begin to share food or drink, provide medical assistance, or teach, counsel, or console. Later He promises that the measure you measure with will be measured back to you. So, if you desire mercy, then be quick to show mercy to others.

"Blessed are the pure in heart, for they shall see God" (Matthew 5:8). Only God can probe the heart and the inner self (Psalm 7:10; Revelation 2:23). Jesus reads the souls of all the people in His audience, and knows what they have inside them. Then He pronounces this blessing upon them. God sees their worth and will one day reward some of them with the beatific vision in return. The Psalms speak of those who are *pure of hands* (Psalm 18:20, 24) innocent of wrongdoing, but also of those who are *pure of heart* (Psalm 24:4; 73:1) innocent of idolatry. Jesus blesses here those whose hearts are so given to God that they would never think of harming another.

"Blessed are the peacemakers, for they shall be called sons of God" (Matthew 5:9). Armed soldiers provide crowd control. Pilgrim bands could get unruly. Samaritan and Jewish pilgrims cross each other on the same roads on the festivals to get to different shrines. Flavius Josephus tells of several riots that began on holy days. Soldiers guard important roads like the one passing through Capernaum, if for no other reason than to keep the tax collectors from being stoned to death. Jesus blesses these officers of the peace, for even though agents of a hated colonial power, they keep the pilgrims safe. The church serves the needs of those who serve in the armed forces, keeping others safe. Martin of Tours, a soldier, put his military cloak on the ground for a beggar, who turned out to be Jesus. Now he is the patron saint of soldiers, and his feast is on Veteran's Day, formerly called Armistice Day, when the First World War ended on November 11, 1918.

"Blessed are those who are persecuted for righteousness' sake, for theirs is the kingdom of heaven" (Matthew 5:10). Verses ten and eleven look like two different beatitudes, but are actually the same; the first is in third person "those" but the second in second person "you." The effect is very dramatic in verse eleven, when the beatitudes become no longer about them but about YOU. The apostles who heard this sermon would be persecuted and many martyred in years to come.

John Chrysostom, schooled in the art of Greek rhetoric says that the *kingdom of heaven*, though not promised in each, and every beatitude, is implied in all of them. The promise is expressed in the first and last beatitudes, forming a rhetorical "inclusion," and thus belongs to every item between them. The whole list of beatitudes is about membership in the kingdom of heaven. Many authors have written insightful and helpful books about the beatitudes. At this moment well over three thousand volumes are in print with that phrase in their titles. If a person read one book per day, it would take nearly ten years to read them all. Maybe people should frequently read and pray the Sermon on the Mount daily.

"You are the salt of the earth" (Matthew 5:13). The sermon continues with two little metaphors that are actually parables. The eight beatitudes divide into eight different, overlapping sections. Now Jesus addresses the entire assembly for the first time, calling them the salt of the earth and light of the world. Elsewhere Jesus calls Himself the Light of the World, but here He uses this term for disciples. The second metaphor explains the first. The salt metaphor is a bit obscure, but the light metaphor is very clear. At the end of the sermon there are two full-blown parables, about the houses built on rock or sand. The two parables here and the two parables there form a framing device, to begin and end the sermon. Most parables survive in a free-floating form, but here in this sermon, one has an opportunity to see how Jesus used the parables in the larger context of his preaching.

"Think not that I have come to abolish the law and the prophets" (Matthew 5:17). Following upon the introduction provided by the Beatitudes and the two little metaphors, Jesus launches into the essence of the sermon with an exposition on four specific commandments of the Torah. Until this moment He has drawn upon the wisdom literature for material, such as Psalm 37, which would put Him on the same level as David and Solomon. Now, however, He begins to process material from the Torah, and He assumes a teaching authority equal to that of Moses.

While Pope Benedict XVI was serving on the throne of Peter, he wrote a great series entitled *Jesus of Nazareth*. In the second volume, he discusses the teaching authority of Jesus. In Hebrew, the word Torah means not "law" but "teaching," although it may contain commandments within it. He calls the first five books of the Old Testament the "Torah of Moses," but he calls the first four books of the New Testament the "Torah of the Messiah." Pope Benedict XVI shows that they do not collide with one another, but merge into a single, coherent Bible.

The Torah of Moses promised both blessings and curses, but for some reason the curses were put down in writing and the blessings were not. There is something left incomplete, perhaps left in the oral sphere and not set down in writing in the Old Testament. The Messiah gives a Torah that expresses the blessings that had been left implied, in a covenant written on hearts and not in stone (Jeremiah 31:31f). After asserting that He plans to fulfill and not destroy, Jesus proceeds to unfold His masterful interpretation of four of the most important Mosaic commandments.

"You shall not kill" (Exodus 20:13, Deuteronomy 5:17, Matthew 5:21). Jesus first tackles the fifth commandment. All termination of human life objectively violates this commandment, even when one is protecting the common good. The Book of Wisdom, contains the remarkable statement: *God did not make death* (Wisdom 1:13). Saint John Paul II spoke eloquently about the "culture of death," which finds lives expendable for the sake of social convenience. Far from dispensing or lightening the commandment, Jesus interiorizes it: *"But I say to you that every one who is angry with his brother shall be liable to judgment"* (Matthew 5:22). People can kill with a word—not the body, but the spirit. So Jesus gives the new commandment not to hate. All acts of violence begin with violent thoughts. All sinful deeds begin as temptations of the mind.

Traditional Catholic teaching left the taking of guilty life to the prudential judgment of lay authority, but banned the taking of innocent life. As collateral damage has become more extensive, however, prudential judgment seems to demand a path of peace. Saint John XXIII said that when humanity has the power to destroy the entire world, war is no longer a reasonable recourse for injustice. Many Catholics seem unaware that this has been settled papal teaching for over fifty years. In 1965 Blessed Paul VI told the United Nations General Assembly, "No more war!" Saint John Paul II told world leaders that they will answer to history, their consciences, and God. Members of the Vatican diplomatic corps try diligently to avert conflicts all over the globe. Peace is not just a pious notion. The Sermon on the Mount has become essential to the survival of life on this planet.

"You shall not commit adultery" (Exodus 20:14, Deuteronomy 5:18, Matthew 5:27). Next, Jesus addresses the thorny question of adultery. Human beings are social in their very nature, and adultery tears at the fabric of our social existence, separating spouses from one another, parents from children, grandparents from their offspring, and children from their inheritance. Going down this road leaves human society a wasteland of lost joys, bad consciences, and foul moral habits.

Jesus uses a Rabbinic method, *gezerah sheba*, interpreting the Torah by the Torah, of prophets by the prophets, and wisdom books by wisdom books. The first five books were considered the writings of Moses, and Jesus uses Genesis, the first book of the Torah, to interpret the later books, pointing back to the primal joy of the Garden of Paradise, before original sin, where one man cohabited with one woman in bliss. Neither of them was ever tempted to adultery, even after the Fall, because there were no other objects for their affection. Adam and Eve were faithful to each other for their long lifetimes, and celebrated six hundred wedding anniversaries together. The Catholic Nuptial Rite praises marriage as the one good that human beings did not lose in the Fall, or find washed away in the flood.

Because of Jesus' great teaching, matrimony has been elevated from the status of a universal basic human good to that of a Sacrament, an outward sign instituted by Christ to give grace, signifying the marriage between Christ and his Church. The Sermon on the Mount gives license for marriage only to one man and one woman, until death do they part. This teaching is not intended to make life difficult, but to prevent the demonstrable damage done when matrimony is violated. When a marriage can be proven to be lacking something essential to its nature, then the Church grants an annulment. This is not the same as a civil annulment, which wipes the marriage from the registry. Church annulments leave the external forum of the failed marriage intact, and preserve the civil rights of offspring.

"You shall not swear falsely" (Leviticus 19:12, Numbers 30:2, Deuteronomy 23:21, Matthew 5:33). Next, Christ the Teacher takes on the question of perjury. No doubt He foresaw how widespread swearing would become in later centuries. For some reason people, particularly English speakers, think that they will not be heard or taken seriously unless they highlight their points with vulgar expressions. Most films released have been laced with profane expressions, and often blaspheme the Name of Jesus. And, Christians tolerate the routine demeaning of our Redeemer, the Name above all names.

Jesus' advice in the Sermon on the Mount is good counsel particularly for us: *"Let what you say be simply 'Yes' or 'No'"* (Matthew 5:37). The Greek literally reads, "Let yes mean yes, and no mean no."

"An eye for an eye and a tooth for a tooth" (Exodus 21:23–24, Leviticus 24:19–20, Deuteronomy 19:21, Matthew 5:38)—the talonic or talionic law attempts to limit compensation to no more than the original injury. If someone takes your eye, you may claim no more than one of his eyes, and may not take his life. In later jurisprudence, this has translated into the assigning of compensatory damages, in a monetary form. So this law is still enforced in tort litigation all over this land. The law appears three times in the Torah, in longer and shorter formulas in Exodus 21:23–24, Leviticus 24:19–20, and Deuteronomy 19:21. This law seeks to prevent excessive forms of punishment, which may be more severe than the crime itself.

Jesus instructs the citizens of His kingdom to forego the compensation that they might have coming to them, and not to take each other to court. One day each person will stand side-by-side before Christ the Judge, who will establish a reign of true justice. In the meantime we cannot ever find perfect justice, but we can seek to perfect our practice of mercy, here and now.

Christ the Teacher concludes the juridical portion of his Sermon by returning to His first definitive ruling, against hatred as a form of murder. He now turns it into a positive commandment: *"Love your enemies and pray for those who persecute you"* (Matthew 5:44). This inclusion wraps up this section by returning to the header. Forgiveness is so fundamental to Christianity that it is inconceivable without it. No other world-religion places forgiveness in so central a role. Many great sentiments can be found among the sages, prophets, seers and mystics of all great world religions, but none of them emphasize forgiveness like Jesus does. He practiced what He preached, and changed the world forever. A young Hindu in India, Mahatma Gandhi read the Sermon on the Mount and decided to try it. He applied the teachings of Jesus and founded the Satyagraha, or non-violent movement. Consequently, India achieved independence from Great Britain and has become the largest democracy in the world, for over sixty years. So the Sermon on the Mount works even for people who do not worship the Teacher. How much more should the worshippers of Jesus give His Sermon a chance!

1. How do people view Jesus as He teaches? CCC 581

2. Matthew names seven mountains, which three are places of teaching for Jesus?

- ☐ The mount of Temptation (Matthew 4:8)
- ☐ The mount of _____ (Matthew 5:1)
- ☐ The mount of Prayer (Matthew 14:23)
- ☐ The mount of Healing (Matthew 15:29)
- ☐ The mount of _____ (Matthew 17:1)
- ☐ The mount of Olives (Matthew 21:1; 24:3; 26:30)
- ☐ The mount of the Ascension of Our Lord (Matthew 28:16).

3. What does the Catechism teach about the Beatitudes? CCC 1716–1718

4. Explain the kingdom of heaven. Matthew 5:3; CCC 543–544, 764

5. What does *pure of heart* mean? Matthew 5:8; CCC 2518–2519

6. Where can Christians find a model? Matthew 5:12, 17; CCC 520

7. How can one become salt and light to the world? Matthew 5:13–16

* Identify some contemporary Christians who live the Beatitudes.

8. Why did Jesus come? How must disciples behave? Matthew 5:17–20

9. How will we ultimately be judged? Matthew 5:21–26; CCC 678

* Do you have a relationship that needs to be healed or improved?

10. What does Jesus say about adultery and divorce? Matthew 5:27–32

** How can you help people heal after the emotional fallout of adultery today?

11. Should you swear oaths? Matthew 5:33–37; James 5:12

12. Explain the Talonic Law.

Exodus 21:23–25	Leviticus 24:19–20	Deuteronomy 19:20–21

13. How should you react to those who hurt you? Matthew 5:39–42

14. What help can you find in Matthew 5:12?

15. How should a Christian treat enemies? Matthew 5:43–45

16. What can you learn from the wisdom of Proverbs 25:21–22?

17. What does Saint Peter teach disciples? 1 Peter 2:19–22

18. Explain what Jesus says in Matthew 5:48. CCC 1693

19. What is our point of reference for Matthew 5:48? CCC 1698

20. To what do all Christians aspire? CCC 2013

* How can you grow in the above? How can you help and support others?

CHAPTER 6

Our Father
Matthew 6

Our Father who art in heaven,
Hallowed be thy name.
Thy kingdom come.
Thy will be done on earth as it is in heaven.
Matthew 6:9–10

"**B**eware of practicing your piety before men" (Matthew 6:1). If Jesus preached the Sermon in April or May, some pilgrims were on their way home from celebrating Passover in Jerusalem, while others were journeying to Jerusalem for Pentecost. Pilgrimage was a public act of piety for Jewish people. Pilgrims were vulnerable to bandits, easy to spot on roadways or camped in byways. The poor begged alms from them, but local believers were eager to protect and help the pilgrims. Pilgrims were practicing piety before men! Jesus teaches them to remain humble, and not to lord it over other travelers. Traveling merchants, marching soldiers, and slouching locals were not inferior to pilgrims. The pilgrim must avoid arousing jealousy, by insinuating that they prayed better, or lived better lives than others.

Jesus and John the Baptist went into the desert for fasting. Their piety was acceptable because they were not fasting to make a public spectacle. The Christian penitential season of Lent imitates Jesus in the desert; originally Lent comprised forty days of fasting, as it still does for Eastern Christians. Jesus often withdrew to pray alone, rather than praying in public, as an example for His followers. In the Sermon on the Mount, Jesus preaches what He has already been practicing.

The great Day of Atonement, a total fast from both food and drink for twenty-four hours is the one big penitential event in Judaism. People often called Yom Kippur simply *the fast* (Acts 27:9). Some Jews did voluntary fasting on other days beyond the legal minimum. Because Pharisees practiced their piety in public, their penitential practices were recorded for posterity. In the parable of the two men who went to the temple to pray, Jesus quotes the Pharisee as boasting, *"I fast twice a week, I give tithes of all that I get"* (Luke 18:12). Rabbinic sources record that the two days for fasting were on Mondays and Thursdays.

When the early church changed the day of worship from Saturday to Sunday, the days of fasting also shifted, to Wednesdays and Fridays. Church laws regarding fast and abstinence go back to earliest times. Today, Catholics observe:
   ✦ Ash Wednesday and Good Friday, days of fast for those in good health ages eighteen to fifty-nine; the two most important penitential days of the Liturgical year, bookend the season of Lent. Fasting here means one full and two light meals and nothing between meals.

+ All Fridays of the year (unless a feast day) those aged fourteen to fifty-nine abstain from meat, since Christ died in the flesh on a Friday. Since 1968, Catholics in the United States are allowed to substitute a different penance for the abstinence from meat on Fridays to recall Our Lord's Passion.
+ Catholics in good health refrain from food and drink for one hour before receiving Holy Communion. More reverential than penitential, this helps one prepare body and soul for the grace of the Sacrament.

Ancient Jews sprinkled their heads with ashes as penance, giving rise to the practice of marking a cross with ashes on a Christian's forehead on Ash Wednesday, the day each year that the gathered faithful hear this portion of the Sermon on the Mount, so that they may remember what true penitence means. The ashes reveal that the bearer admits sinfulness, needing to repent and be forgiven just as much as the next person. As pleasure and satisfaction are a driving force behind work and play, ashes—a witness of sacrifice provides an example in proclaiming the gospel.

Once some Native Americans came to the local parish church to receive ashes, and asked the priest, "What do the ashes mean?" He answered, "Ashes are peace paint. Just as the warrior puts on war paint to go on the war path, so the prayer warrior puts on ashes to embark on the path of peace." While not an exhaustive answer to the question, other right answers could be given, because a sign like ashes has multiple layers of meaning. Just saying, "I am a Catholic and I want to make a good Lent" provides an excellent reason to get ashes on Ash Wednesday.

"And when you pray, you must not be like the hypocrites" (Matthew 6:5). Christ the Teacher moves from the subject of fasting to the subject of prayer, making a similar point. To pray only for an audience, is like an actor on a stage; therefore private prayer must supplement public prayer. Even a short time alone with God can restore authenticity to our communal prayer life. Take time at the end of Mass to give thanks to God for the Blessed Sacrament received.

In a small rural parish, people all kneel at the end of the Mass for a moment of silent prayer. When the Bishop came for Confirmation, he stood in the back of the church to greet the parishioners, and they all knelt down facing the Tabernacle for about five minutes. He asked the pastor, "What are they doing?" Of course, he was pleased to see their habit of prayer. Apparently the giving of personal thanks is not so common among Catholics that bishops rarely see it done.

The body of Christ is still learning how to pray—the Mass in the vernacular, struggling to develop an appropriate set of hymns, learning to pray the Liturgy of Hours (which once was only for priests and monks), striving to find time for family prayer, and personal prayer, away from the infernal screens that are everywhere. One bishop came to a parish, sat in the parlor with the pastor, and suddenly noticed that there was no television. The pastor said, "I got rid of TV. It was bad for my prayer life." Of course, the bishop was pleased with that answer.

While discussing prayer, at this climactic point in the Sermon on the Mount, Jesus gives the familiar form of the Lord's Prayer, or "Our Father." He starts with: *"do not heap up empty phrases as the Gentiles do"* (Matthew 6:7). No first century pagan prayer from the region of Galilee remains today, so His reference point of contrast has been lost. Five centuries before, however, in his treatise on rhetoric, Aristotle condemned the duplication of words as an abuse, called *battologia* (hitting something again and again). Jesus' instruction corresponds to the teaching of Greek and Roman rhetoricians, avoiding repetition for its own sake. Jesus formulates a prayer using such economy of means that it serves every Christian until the end of time.

"Our Father who art in heaven" (Matthew 6:9a)—Christ the Teacher begins His prayer by invoking His Father, and inviting those who follow Him to address His Father as their own. This particular phrase "Father in heaven" has high importance, mentioned both at the head of this prayer and nine times in all throughout the Sermon on the Mount (Matthew 5:16, 45, 48, 6:1, 9, 14, 26; 7:11, 21). The Collects (opening prayers) of the Roman Missal frequently invoke God under many descriptive titles—Almighty ever-living God, Almighty and merciful God, God of everlasting mercy, God of might, Giver of every good gift, O God from whom all good things come, hope and light of the sincere, Author of our freedom and our salvation, strength of those who hope in you.

Thirty-one psalms begin invoking God by name (YHWH); three psalms address Him with the simple word for God (El), and twenty-one psalms by the more dynamic form (Elohim). Other psalms begin with a rich variety of appellations—God of Justice (Psalm 4), Adonai (Psalm 8, 90), My Strength (Psalm 18), My God my God (Psalm 22), My Rock (Psalm 28), Shepherd of Israel (Psalm 80), Lord Sabaoth (Psalm 84), Lord God of Salvation (Psalm 88), God of My Praises (Psalm 109), and My God the King (Psalm 145). None of the psalms invoke God as Father in the opening words, but one psalm compares God to a human father: *As a father pities his children, so the Lord pities those who fear him* (Psalm 103:13). God the Son uses language like this to invite us all to join him in invoking God the Father. Consequently Christianity has developed an entire spirituality of sonship.

"Hallowed be thy name" (Matthew 6:9b). The first half of the Lord's Prayer gives glory to God—it prays for the hallowing of God's name, the coming of God's kingdom, and the fulfillment of God's will on earth as it is in heaven. The construction here is distinctly Semitic. Jesus certainly taught this prayer in Aramaic, and the Antiochene Christians of the East still pray it in a late form of that language, called Syriac. Scholars have retranslated the prayer back into the first century Palestinian form of Aramaic, and it fits like a hand in glove.

The logic of the prayer would make more sense in Greek, Latin or English if it had been presented as a logical syllogism:
   + God's will, Name, and kingdom, are already realized perfectly in heaven.
   + They are still realized only imperfectly on earth.
   + May the earthly realization rise to the level of the heavenly reality.

People may fear the coming of the kingdom of God, because it will change the familiar order of things. The general public, and even many Christians, fear the end of the world, because of the accompanying tribulations. Christians should think about what they pray so often in the Lord's Prayer: "Thy kingdom come." Perhaps people fear that their personal verdicts may go bad in the final judgment. Jesus gave the antidote for these fears with the following prayer: "Thy will be done." If we do the will of God as best we can in our ordinary daily lives, we need not fear the final judgment. God is coming with judgment in favor of His people, with justice for the innocent who have been wrongly condemned, and with joy for all those who have suffered for the sake of the kingdom.

"Give us this day our daily bread" (Matthew 6:11). In the second half of the Lord's Prayer, Jesus teaches us how to ask the Father for things needed most—daily bread, the ability to forgive, deliverance from temptation and evil. The Hebrews in the desert received daily bread, gathering just enough manna from the desert floor each morning to provide them with food for the day. They could not store the manna overnight, except for the double portion on Friday morning, which served the people for two days, over the sabbath, and a tiny portion that was reserved permanently in the Ark of the Covenant. After the donation of the prayer, Jesus will develop the notion of not hoarding during the rest of chapter six.

On one level the term daily bread means physical bread for the hungry, because Jesus did multiply loaves for the multitude on more than one occasion. Feeding the hungry is a corporal work of mercy. On a deeper level, Jesus offers spiritual bread for the soul, the Eucharist. Manna in the desert was a sign that God was caring for His people on their way to the Holy Land, and the Blessed Sacrament provides God's gift of spiritual nourishment on the pilgrim path to Heaven. The Daily Bread will give us the strength to forgive others, resist temptation and avoid evil.

How many Christians realize that praying the Lord's Prayer gives God permission to condemn us, unless we have forgiven one another? The prayer is like an oath: "I promise to forgive, or may God leave me in my sins!" Forgiveness is the virtue most at the heart of the kingdom of God, because God the Son came to earth precisely for the purpose of forgiving all the sinners of all time. Forgiven of our offences against Almighty God, we must now pass on forgiveness in kind to others. We must not be only consumers of mercy but also producers of mercy, no matter how difficult it may be.

The last two importations are liberating. We are not left to our own devices to resist temptation, but we implore the grace of God for such moments. With that grace we will walk through brambles without pain, and walk through the seabed dry-shod. Finally, the same Jesus who tells us to resist evil also teaches us to implore His Father that we may be delivered from it. If the Father so wills, evil cannot touch us. In Luke, the donation of the Lord's Prayer took place after one of the disciples came and asked, *"Lord, teach us to pray, as John taught his disciples"* (Luke 11:1). The disciple may have been Andrew, who had been following John the Baptist before he met Jesus. No prayers of John the Baptist remain, but the first half of the Lord's Prayer has a number of elements common to the preaching of John. Possibly the first half of the Lord's Prayer was what John the

Baptist taught his disciples, and the Lord may have built upon that by adding His own characteristic approach in the second half.

Matthew's Lord's Prayer is longer than Luke's. The *Didache*, or "Teaching of the Twelve Apostles to the Nations" is even longer. The Didache, lost for centuries, was rediscovered in 1873 in Constantinople. Scholars date it to the second half of the first century, making it the earliest known Christian writing outside the New Testament. The Didache version, found in the Byzantine manuscript tradition of Matthew, is not found in the earliest and best, Alexandrian manuscript tradition of Matthew. Scholars accept the ending as authentic ancient prayer, but not as part of the version transmitted by Matthew himself.

The Lord's Prayer continues to unite Christians of all denominations and rites. The Didache says that Christians should pray this prayer three times per day. In fact, the Church continues to do this, at the daily Liturgies of Morning Prayer (Lauds), Eucharist (Mass) and Evening Prayer (Vespers).

The Lord's Prayer

Luke 11:2–4	Matthew 6:9–13	Didache
Father,	Our Father Who art in heaven,	Our Father, Who art in heaven,
Hallowed be your name. Your kingdom come.	Hallowed be thy name. Thy kingdom come, Thy will be done On earth as it is in heaven.	Hallowed be thy name. Thy kingdom come.

Give us each day our daily bread;
and forgive us our sins,
for we ourselves forgive every one
   who is indebted to us,
and lead us not into temptation.
	Give us this day our daily bread;
	And forgive us our trespasses
	As we forgive those who trespass
	   against us;
	And lead us not into temptation,
	But deliver us from evil.
		Give us this day our daily bread;
		And forgive us our debt
		   as we also forgive those
		   who trespass against us;
		and lead us not into temptation,
		But deliver us from evil.

		For thine is the power and the glory for ever.

"Do not lay up for yourselves treasures on earth" (Matthew 6:19). The injunction against hoarding things hearkens back to the first of the beatitudes, "Blessed are the poor." Grinding poverty often teaches poor people to save what they have and not to waste. Some survivors of the Great Depression became compulsive hoarders, because they feared a desperate time like that might come again. Still, that generation gave generously to educate their children, and to support their church.

Diocesan priests do not take a vow of poverty, because they live in the world to minister to the laity. Diocesan priests receive salaries and pay taxes just like other citizens. The charism of celibacy enables priests to function at a very low salary. Four hundred thousand men are giving up having families of their own to serve a billion Catholics throughout the world. Most third-world dioceses are too poor to provide any salary at all, and their clergy must live on gifts. A salary is better, because the priest belongs to all the people and not just to a few.

All the faithful are called to participate in the kingdom of God through works of corporal and spiritual mercy. Consequently, lay people embrace a special spirituality of stewardship, with their financial assets. By their generosity, they make possible all the good works of the church. To donate even a little, is better than nothing at all. Traditionally, parishioners have been encouraged to give five percent of their income to the parish and five percent to other worthy charities.

"Consider the lilies of the field" (Matthew 6:28). If the Sermon on the Mount took place between Passover and Pentecost, in May, then lilies were blooming on the hillsides within full view of Jesus and His audience on that spring morning. If so, then the image of the lilies of the field was not merely a mental construction, but attached a spiritual meaning to what lay before the eyes of everyone present.

Lilium martagon, which grows from Portugal to Mongolia was probably growing on the slopes of the Mount of Beatitudes. The typically pinkish purple color resembles the purple robes worn by Roman nobility. The Greek text of Matthew uses the word *ta krina*, plural of *to krinon*. In the actual sermon, Jesus most likely used the Hebrew word *shoshan*. Hosea says of the Messiah that he *will blossom as the lily* (Hosea 14:5), and the Song of Songs says that the bridegroom is like *a lily of the valleys* and will grow *as a lily among brambles* (Song of Solomon 2:1, 2).

Plant similes occur with some frequency in the Book of Psalms. The wicked are like chaff blowing in the wind (Psalm 1:4, 35:5). People blossom for a short season but then they wither like green vines (Psalm 37:2), like plants (Psalm 72:16, 92:7, 102:4, 11), like the grass (Psalm 37:2, 90:5, 103:15, 129:6). The just man is like a tree planted by running streams (Psalm 1:3), like an olive tree in the house of God (Psalm 52:8). The just man's children are like olive shoots (Psalm 128:3), for his wife is like a fruitful vine in the recesses of their home (Psalm 128:3).

Jesus draws upon this rich heritage of floral imagery, particularly from Psalm 37, which already contributed one of the eight beatitudes when the Sermon began. The comparison to lilies, however, goes beyond any source material, making a Messianic statement, for he praises the beauty of nature as outstripping even the royal robes of Solomon. Jesus, rightful heir to the throne of David, points out that the historical Kingdom of Israel had a manufactured magnificence; the throne to which He aspires belongs to the kingdom of Heaven, which is not of this world. Dante Alighieri was inspired by such imagery to picture Heaven itself as a gigantic white rose, symbolizing divine love, the petals of which are the souls of the faithful. Special place there belongs to the Queen of Heaven:

"O Virgin Mother, O daughter of your own Son!
. . . In your womb there reignited the Love,
by whose heat, by such means
this flower has blossomed unto eternal peace."
(Paradiso, Canto XXXIII)

1. What can you learn about practicing penance?

Matthew 6:1–4
CCC 1430
CCC 1436

* Which penitential practices do you regularly embrace?

2. What can you learn about prayer?

Matthew 6:5–7
CCC 2608
CCC 2655

3. Where should one go to pray?

Matthew 6:6
CCC 2691

* Where do you like to go for personal prayer?

4. How significant to the Christian is the Lord's Prayer? Matthew 6:9–13

CCC 2759
CCC 2776

5. For what is the Christian desiring and praying?

Matthew 6:10
CCC 2632

6. Explain the following passages.

Matthew 6:11
CCC 1324
CCC 2659

* Share the importance of the Eucharist in your personal life.

7. Use a dictionary or the Catechism to define "forgiveness."

8. Why is forgiveness essential?

Matthew 6:12
CCC 2845

** Is there anyone you have been unable to forgive? Pray for the grace to forgive.

9. Explain Matthew 6:13, using these passages.

John 17:15
James 1:13–15
CCC 2846–2847
CCC 2848

*** What common temptations face people in your age group?

10. What are the rewards of forgiving others, even if they don't deserve it?

Matthew 6:14
Ephesians 4:31–32
Colossians 3:12–13

11. What happens to one who refuses to forgive another? Matthew 6:15

12. What happens when you pray the "Our Father?" Matthew 6:9–13

CCC 2789
CCC 2792

13. Use a dictionary or the Catechism to define "fasting."

14. What can you learn about fasting?

Matthew 6:16–18
CCC 1434
CCC 2043

15. What can you learn about treasures?

Matthew 6:19–21
1 Timothy 6:17–19

16. What is the light of the soul? Matthew 6:22–23

17. Who is your Master? Matthew 6:24

* How much time do you spend on Him?

18. Why should you not worry? Who takes care of your needs?

Matthew 6:25–32
CCC 270

19. What should you do instead of worrying? Matthew 6:33

20. When should you concern yourself?

Matthew 6:34
CCC 2836

Monthly Social Activity

This month, your small group will meet for coffee, tea, or a simple breakfast, lunch, or dessert in someone's home. Pray for this social event and for your host or hostess. Try, if at all possible, to attend.

Jesus began to preach, saying, "Repent, for the kingdom of heaven is at hand" (Matthew 4:17).

Reflect on this and recall a time that you felt called to repent, turn to God and follow Jesus more closely.

Some examples:

✤ *I reached a bad place in my life, and had nowhere else to turn. So, I turned back to God, and went to Confession.*

✤ *A friend invited me to a Prayer Meeting. I went and experienced the presence of God.*

✤ *The parish bulletin advertised a Bible Study. I had never studied God's Word, so I decided to give it a try.*

CHAPTER 7

The Narrow Gate
Matthew 7

Enter by the narrow gate;
for the gate is wide and the way is easy, that leads to destruction,
and those who enter by it are many.
For the gate is narrow and the way is hard,
that leads to life, and those who find it are few.
Matthew 7:13–14

Christ the Teacher now brings to a conclusion His greatest surviving Sermon. An excellent homily requires three things—a beginning, middle, and end. This sermon has the best beginning (The Beatitudes), the best middle (The Lord's Prayer), and now the best possible ending (the double parable of the house built on rock or sand). No other teacher has ever left behind such a manifesto, so moving, and so well constructed.

In Byzantine iconography, Jesus sometimes appears as Christos Didascalos, Christ the Teacher, blessing people with His right hand while holding an open book in His left, with New Testament verses that can be read, such as *"I am the Alpha and the Omega, the beginning and the end"* (Revelation 21:6) in the Cloister of Sant' Angelo, or *"I am the light of the world"* (John 8:12) in the Cathedral of Cefalù.

Christ usually assumes a standing posture in these icons, but in one Albanian icon He is seated, with the book spread open in His lap. Sitting was the normal posture assumed by Greek philosophers, Jewish rabbis, and ancient kings, while their students and courtiers stood. On the Mount of Beatitudes Jesus sat, but many people in the crowd stood so that they could see and hear Him better.

Some scholars think that Matthew constructed this sermon in its present form out of segments of material, some of which appear in Mark and Luke. Others believe that the Sermon on the Mount paints a more accurate picture of how Jesus preached. Before a large crowd, eager to listen and learn, He would hardly limit Himself to lectionary-sized sound bites. Once-in-a-lifetime pilgrims came from afar, hoping to hear Jesus, John the Baptist, and others preach in the land, so they could report back to their family and friends. Well-motivated audiences could easily handle hours of oratory. Jesus no doubt gave many lengthy discourses.

Jesus had so much to say, and so little time in which to teach. At the beginning of the Sermon on the Mount, the whole human race was still in a spiritual kindergarten, except for the Jews, who had advanced several grades. In the short span of three years, Jesus would have to communicate enough of His message so that the Church could get a firm grip and keep hold of it until the end of time.

"Judge not, that you may be not judged" (Matthew 7:1). People misuse this verse to tolerate serious sin. Yet, Jesus also says, *"Do not judge by appearances, but judge with right judgment"* (John 7:24). Everyone must make prudential judgments every day. Some acts are good; others evil. Choose to do this, or not. *Open your mouth, judge righteously* (Proverbs 31:9). Here, Jesus warns against condemning another, or presuming to know another's heart. God is the final judge of all. When comparing incomplete human knowledge with the infinite wisdom of God, human judgments fall short. Jesus warns His followers not to presume too much. Rather than condemning someone who is in serious sin, take courage and *speak the truth in love* (Ephesians 4:15). Never condone sin. Never condemn a sinner. Lead sinners back. *Whoever brings back a sinner from the error of his way will save his soul from death and will cover a multitude of sins* (James 5:20).

The Sermon on the Mount provides the pedagogical foundation of the entire New Testament. The the Letter of James has much in common with Matthew's Gospel. On the subject of judging, for example, James says extensively: *"Do not speak evil against one another, brethren. He that speaks evil against a brother or judges his brother, speaks evil against the law and judges the law. But if you judge the law, you are not a doer of the law but a judge . . . whoever brings back a sinner from the error of his way will save his soul from death."* (James 4:11; 5:20).

"Do not give dogs what is holy; and do not throw your pearls before swine, lest they trample them under foot and turn to attack you" (Matthew 7:6). So, do not perform to a hostile audience. Elsewhere, Jesus instructs the disciples to shake the dust off their feet and leave any town that will not receive them (Matthew 10:14). Matthew 7:6 relates better to the preceding verses about the speck and beam, than to the following verses about fruitful prayer. If this saying relates to making judgments, why would Christians talk judgmentally about others in public places? Each and every person is a holy pearl for whom Jesus gave His lifeblood. If people are trampled underfoot like swine, and turn against others like dogs, how can we ever draw other people to God's mercy and the saving sacraments? Nothing undermines evangelism more than when those initiated into grace indulge in demeaning talk.

The first century document, the *Didache* gives this application: "But let no one eat or drink of your Eucharist, except those baptized into the name of the Lord; for as regards this also the Lord has said: Give not that which is holy to the dogs." We all must rise above our lower natures to prepare ourselves properly for Communion— first through Baptism, then through Confession at least once a year and more often as needed, then through an hour of fasting and prayer. Those who feel drawn to the altar must leave behind the old self.

"Ask, and it will be given to you" (Matthew 7:7). Jesus recapitulates themes in the last part of the Sermon, in fresh ways. He speaks vividly again about the importance of persistence in prayer. One person stands outside a house and does not knock; a second knocks politely, and then walks away; a third knocks persistently. The probabilities of that door opening are unlikely for the first, better for the second, and best for the third. The same thing must

be true of prayer. Elsewhere Jesus makes the same point by means of the Parable of the Unjust Judge (Luke 18:1–9), assailed in his home by the poor widow demanding justice.

Imagine a house of many doors, all barred but one. People come and examine all the doors, but refuse to enter unless the door they like opens for them. Meanwhile, one door stands wide open. Some people complain that prayer is never answered, because it is not answered the way they think it should be. Every prayer is answered, sometimes in surprising ways, sometimes in ways unknown. It is always good to ask, because those who do not ask are burying a God-given talent.

Saint Ambrose of Milan compared the Book of Psalms to a great house with many doors. Psalm One is the door for the just man: *He is like a tree planted by streams of water, that yields its fruit in its season, and its leaf does not wither. In all that he does, he prospers* (Psalm 1:3), which corresponds to the petition "Give us this day our daily bread." Another good entry point is the conclusion of Psalm 24: *Lift up your heads, O gates! and be lifted up, O ancient doors! that the King of glory may come in. Who is this King of glory? The Lord of hosts, he is the King of glory* (Psalm 24:9–10). This matches the petition "Thy kingdom come."

Saint James continues to expound upon the efficacy of prayer in his letter. *If any of you lacks wisdom, let him ask God, who gives to all men generously and without reproaching, and it will be given him. But let him ask in faith, with no doubting, for he who doubts is like a wave of the sea that is driven and tossed by the wind* (James 1:5–6). He also writes: *Every good endowment and every perfect gift is from above, coming down from the Father of lights with whom there is no variation or shadow due to change* (James 1: 17). Pray fervently and persistently.

"So whatever you wish that men would do to you, do so to them; for this is the law and the prophets" (Matthew 7:12). Jesus took a Golden Rule found in Scripture (Tobit 4:15; Sirach 31:15) and used it as the interpretive key to His Sermon. Who wants to be hated, killed, cheated, or left unforgiven? Who wants to be looked down upon by others? Who wants to be judged? Jesus also cites this rule in His Sermon on the Plain (Luke 6:31). Other Rabbis also taught the Golden Rule, for it entered into the Talmud in a prescriptive form: "That which is hateful to you, do not to your fellow. That is the whole Torah; the rest is the explanation; go and learn it" (the "Great Principle" in Talmud Shabbat 31a).

Commentators identify the Golden Rule as based closely upon the second of the great commandments, *"Love your neighbor as yourself"* (Leviticus 19:18), but both Jesus and the Talmud reveal that it expresses the whole Torah. Thus in the broadest sense the Golden Rule governs our relationship with God as well. If you were God, how would you like to be treated? Would you like the creatures you have made to disown you, curse you, take your gifts thanklessly, ignore your commandments and misuse your created world? If you were Jesus, would you like to be named in vain, doubted, disbelieved, crowned with thorns, scourged, nailed to a cross and pierced by a sword, by the very people that you came to earth to save? Try to put yourself in His shoes. Give to Jesus the honor He deserves.

"Enter by the narrow gate" (Matthew 7:13). Important people choose the wide gate, but marginalized people slip in through humble passageways. The narrow gate that Jesus models is the gate of humility. By His suffering, death and Resurrection, Jesus opens the gate to the kingdom of heaven to those who will repent of their sins, believe in Him, and accept baptism. *Open to me the gates of righteousness, that I may enter through them and give thanks to the LORD. This is the gate of the LORD; the righteous shall enter through it* (Psalm 118:19–20).

At funerals today, whether of a drug lord or a saintly grandfather, you will hear mourners declare: "he is in a better place!" Contemporary people assign everyone to heaven. They presume that if hell exists, probably no one goes there, except maybe mass murderers. But, contemporary assumptions are exactly the opposite of Jesus' words and admonition! Jesus warns that the way to hell is broad and easy, and many are on their way to destruction! *The way of the wicked will perish* (Psalm 1:6). The way to eternal life is narrow and hard. Do not be surprised at trials and hardships. Never stop sharing the good news of God's mercy with those who are on the wide path. Never say, "Who am I to judge?" while a loved one plunges into spiritual darkness and doom. Pray, speak the truth in love, and offer Masses for the souls of deceased loved ones, who may still be in Purgatory.

> "He *[Justice Antonin Scalia]* wrote: 'Even when the deceased was an admirable person, indeed especially when the deceased was an admirable person, praise for his virtues can cause us to forget that we are praying for and giving thanks for God's inexplicable mercy to a sinner.' Now, he would not have exempted himself from that. We are here, then, as he would want: to pray for God's inexplicable mercy to a sinner. Let us not show him a false love, and allow our admiration to deprive him of our prayers. We continue to show affection for him and do good for him by praying for him, that all stain of sin be washed away, that all sins be healed, that he be purified of all that is not Christ."
>
> (Father Paul Scalia, *Homily*, February 20, 2016)

"Not every one who says to me 'Lord, Lord,' shall enter the kingdom of heaven" (Matthew 7:21). Jesus demands more than a profession of faith and lip service from His followers; He also demands that faith be put into action. The whole New Testament teaches this, especially the Gospel of Matthew and the Letter of James. *"But be doers of the word, and not hearers only, deceiving yourselves* (James 1:22). Even Paul sees faith as the means, and love as the goal (1 Corinthians 13).

Jesus illustrates genuine faith with a double parable, the first true parable that appears in Matthew's Gospel. Two little metaphors in Matthew 5 took the form, *"You are the salt of the earth. . . . You are the light of the world"* (Matthew 5:13–14). Here, however, the comparison is expressed with use of the word "like," in the form of a simile: *"Every one then who hears these words of mine and does them will be like a wise man who built his house upon the rock"* (Matthew 7:24). The comparison is also stated conversely, making the parable doubled. We must build upon God's Word.

Jesus began the Sermon on the Mount with the Beatitudes, and His concluding parable gives a beatitude in disguise—blessed is the one who hears these words and does them. Jesus went up the mountain, near to heaven and to God the Father, to challenge His disciples and the entire world with a whole new way of defining blessedness. He had no intention of letting people ignore His words. So now the concluding challenge—do something! Put words into action! Build the house of your life upon the rock of His Word! Stay on the narrow path that leads to life.

1. What can you learn from these passages?

Leviticus 19:15–16
Proverbs 31:9
Matthew 7:1–5
John 7:24

2. Who will be the ultimate judge?

Isaiah 33:22
John 5:28–30
CCC 679

* Are you inclined to be judgmental, or to be silent, when you should speak up?

3. Who helps you recognize your own *(log in your eye)* faults? Matthew 7:3

4. Who can help you correct your sins and amend your life? Matthew 7:5

5. Explain Matthew 7:6 in your own words.

6. Compare the following verses.

Matthew 7:7–8
John 15:7–8
James 4:3
1 John 3:21–22

7. What can you learn about intercessory prayer?

Matthew 7:8–11
CCC 2609, 2611
CCC 2821, 2826

8. From where does everything come? James 1:16–18

9. What can you learn from the following passages?

Leviticus 19:17–18
Sirach 31:15
CCC 1970

10. Explain the rule found in Matthew 7:12. CCC 1789

11. Find the moral of the following passages.

Deuteronomy 30:19–20
Wisdom 5:6–7
CCC 1696

12. Is hell real?

Matthew 7:13; 25:41, 46
CCC 1034–1037

13. What warning does Jesus give in Matthew 7:15?

14. What do those who stay on the narrow path experience?

Matthew 7:14
CCC 1821

15. How can you discern truth from falsehood? 1 Thessalonians 5:21–22

16. What helps discern good fruit? Matthew 7:19–20; CCC 2005

17. Explain the following directives.

Matthew 7:21
CCC 2611, 2826

18. How do you know the "will of the Father" for your life? CCC 1780

19. Explain the parable in Matthew 7:24–27 in your own words.

20. Why were the crowds astonished? Matthew 7:28–29

* What helps you stay on the narrow path? Are you surprised when it is hard?

CHAPTER 8

Jesus Heals
Matthew 8–9

*But the centurion answered him
"Lord, I am not worthy to have you come under my roof;
but only say the word, and my servant will be healed."*
Matthew 8:8

Healing miracles of Jesus—fulfill the Messianic prophecy of Isaiah: *"Behold, your God will come with vengeance, with the recompense of God. He will come and save you." Then the eyes of the blind shall be opened, and the ears of the deaf unstopped; then shall the lame man leap like a deer, and the tongue of the mute sing for joy* (Isaiah 35:4–6). As Exodus reports ten plagues inflicted upon the Egyptians, Matthew weaves reports of ten miracles of Jesus in three segments, separated by three teachings about discipleship.

Jesus Heals Leprosy	(Matthew 8:1–4)	
Heals Paralysis	(Matthew 8:5–13)	
Heals a Fever	(Matthew 8:14–17)	
	Cost of Discipleship	(Matthew 8:18–22)
Rebukes a Storm	(Matthew 8:23–27)	
Delivers Demons	(Matthew 8:28–34)	
Heals a Paralytic	(Matthew 9:1–8)	
	Call of Matthew	(Matthew 9:9–13)
	Questions on Fasting	(Matthew 9:14–17)
Cures Hemorrhage	(Matthew 9:20–22)	
Raises the Dead	(Matthew 9:23–26)	
Heals Blindness	(Matthew 9:27–31)	
Heals Muteness	(Matthew 9:32–34)	

Leprosy *(Hansen's Disease)*, a deadly, disfiguring, highly contagious disease, was incurable until the mid-twentieth century. This chronic bacterial disease caused by *mycobacterium leprae* required strict isolation. Father Damien (Josef DeVeuster 1840–1889) of Belgium, volunteered to minister to the leper colony on the island of Molokai, Hawaii, where he contracted and died of leprosy with the lepers he served. Pope Benedict XVI canonized Saint Damien of Molokai in October 2009.

Contact with a leper risks contracting the disease, and makes an observant Jew ritually impure. This leper approaches Jesus in profound humility, kneels down, and acknowledges that Jesus has the power to heal him, if it is God's will. Jesus could easily cure the leper with a *word*. But, amazingly, Jesus *touches* the leper. Instead of the leprosy making Jesus ritually unclean, Jesus' power and holiness makes the leper clean. Telling the leper to show himself to the priest, demonstrates Jesus' observance of Mosaic Law and His respect for the priesthood.

Centurion's prayer—This Gentile military officer, in charge of one hundred foot soldiers, maintained the Roman presence in the area. The Greek word *pais* could be translated as "boy," which could indicate either a servant or a son. Jesus agrees to go with the centurion to heal this boy. But, the response of the centurion shows humility and courtesy, sensitive to the fact that observant Jews do not enter the homes of Gentiles. The power of Jesus' *word* heals the boy. *God's Word* has power! *He sent forth his word, and healed them* (Psalm 107:20). *It was your word, O LORD, which heals all men* (Wisdom 16:12). Jesus is amazed at the faith of this centurion. This represents the only time in Matthew's Gospel that Jesus shows amazement. Later, others will be amazed at the miraculous works and words of Jesus, but here Jesus is amazed at such strong faith.

The Eucharistic Liturgy adopts the words of the centurion immediately prior to the faithful receiving Holy Communion—"Lord, I am not worthy that you should enter under my roof, but only say the word and my soul shall be healed." Believers thus demonstrate humility in approaching the altar of the Lord, and faith in the truth of Jesus' words: *"This is my body"* (Matthew 26:26). The Blessed Sacrament heals the soul and provides the medicine of immortality—the Body, Blood, Soul, and Divinity of Jesus.

When Jesus enters Peter's house, He recognizes that Peter's mother-in-law is sick, but no one asks Him to heal her. Jesus sees her suffering, and His healing touch causes her fever to vanish. Restored to good health, she promptly resumes her role and the dignity of active service in the body of Christ.

Discipleship—Following this first triad of healing miracles, a scribe and a disciple offer to follow Jesus. But, they have reservations, and procrastinate. Jesus honestly relates that His kingdom will not offer the political and economic security that many seek. Discipleship requires sacrifice and an itinerant way of life, relying on the Heavenly Father to provide shelter, strength, and sustenance. Here, for the first time, Jesus identifies Himself as the *"Son of man"* (Matthew 8:20), which will appear repeatedly in Matthew's Gospel. Jesus insists that Christian discipleship must take precedence, even above family and other genuine concerns. To follow Jesus one must be willing to forsake all else. Are you a true disciple of Jesus? Are you "all in?" Or are you still on the fence, a fair-weather friend of Jesus?

Nature obeys God—Storms often occur at sea, especially on the Sea of Galilee. However, Matthew uses the Greek word *seismos,* which actually means an "earthquake." This word also foretells the horrors of the last days, preceding the coming of Christ in Glory. Suffice it to say, that the disciples in the boat are in a catastrophic situation, and they know it. Jesus sleeps in the boat (Matthew 8:24), just as Jonah was fast asleep in the boat during his tempest at sea (Jonah 1:5). The disciples wake Jesus with a prayer. *"Save us, Lord; we are perishing"* (Matthew 8:25). This remains a perfect prayer of the persecuted Church of all ages, tossed about in a chaotic world. "Lord, save us, we are lost." Safety and security for believers entails staying in the barque of Peter—the Catholic Church—where Jesus promised to remain with us until the end of the age (Matthew 28:20).

Heed warnings. In 2005, Hurricane Katrina hit the United States, causing a total of almost two thousand deaths, and 108 billion dollars of damage. Many deaths occurred because people failed to heed warnings to evacuate. People had endured storms before, and chose to ride it out. How bad could it be? Hence, the Coast Guard rescued 34,000 people in New Orleans alone! Following the disaster, someone suggested that scientists shoot pellets into the eye of a hurricane to diminish the force! Is it so hard for people to accept that only God can control nature? Those who experience a tornado, flood, hurricane, or other natural disaster develop a healthy respect for nature, and man's inability to subdue it.

The Psalmist knows that God has power over nature. *You rule the raging of the sea; when its waves rise, you still them* (Psalm 89:9). *They cried to the LORD in their trouble, and he delivered them from their distress; he made the storm be still, and the waves of the sea were hushed* (Psalm 107:28–29). God controls nature. When Jesus rebukes the wind and sea, nature obeys Him. The sudden great calm alarms the disciples, who ask, *"What sort of man is this, that even winds and sea obey him?"* (Matthew 8:27). What sort of man has the power to control nature? Only the God-man, Jesus the Christ, true God and true man, holds such amazing power.

Jesus overpowers demons—in Gadara, a city of the Decapolis, a predominantly a Gentile town populated by Greeks, which the Romans placed under Syrian control. Possession by evil spirits emerges clearly in the Bible. Demons torment people and make their lives, and their loved ones miserable. Here, the demons, who *do* torment people, project their bad behavior onto Jesus, Who they correctly identify. *"What have you to do with us, O Son of God? Have you come here to torment us before the time?"* (Matthew 8:29). Later, Jesus pronounces the punishment for them at His Second Coming and Judgment. *"Depart from me, you cursed, into the eternal fire prepared for the devil and his angels"* (Matthew 25:41). Jesus has power even over Satan and his minions, and they know it.

Jesus heals body and soul. When Jesus meets a paralytic, He sees more than a medical problem. Sin produces spiritual disease and eternal death. Contemporary people spend fortunes on health food to preserve physical wellbeing, while often ignoring spiritual cancers. Jesus has the power to forgive sins and restore spiritual health. Jesus says, *"Take heart, my son; your sins are forgiven"* (Matthew 9:2). Some of the scribes think that Jesus is blaspheming, for only God can forgive sins. But, Jesus knows their thoughts, and that they have evil in their hearts. Who can read minds and discern hearts? *"For the LORD sees not as man sees; man looks on the outward appearance, but the LORD looks on the heart"* (1 Samuel 16:7). Jesus, using logic with the scribes, asks *which is easier, to say, 'Your* *sins are forgiven,' or to say, 'Rise and walk'?* (Matthew 9:5). It is easier to say, *'Your sins are forgiven,'* because no human can evaluate the result. But, if you say, *'Rise and walk'* everyone can see the outcome. Jesus has power over both the physical and the spiritual. It should be obvious. But, they accuse Jesus of blasphemy—a false accusation—for Jesus *is* God. He will ultimately be crucified for the false charge of blasphemy.

Following this triad of healings, Matthew buffers the report with a biographical account. Rabbis saw tax collectors in the same light as robbers and murderers. So, it is astonishing, that Matthew so easily reports his collaboration with the forces of oppression. Matthew may have heard Jesus preaching and teaching earlier. Now, Jesus approaches Matthew, sitting at his tax office, and offers a simple invitation, *"Follow me." And he rose and followed him* (Matthew 9:9). Matthew did not hesitate, and neither should we.

Table fellowship suggests acceptance. Matthew provides only one account of Jesus dining with sinners (Matthew 9:10), but it may have been a common practice for Jesus. Dining with sinners reveals important truths. First, Jesus came to redeem sinners and heal Israel. Secondly, if Jesus eats with Gentiles, then in the early Church, Jewish Christians can share meals with Gentile Christians, as well.

Jesus fasted for forty days in the wilderness, prior to His active ministry (Matthew 4:2). So, He is well acquainted with fasting, although there is no evidence that He demanded any specific fasting from His disciples. Just as God identified as the bridegroom of Israel: *as the bridegroom rejoices over the bride, so shall your God rejoice over you* (Isaiah 62:5b), here Jesus identifies Himself as the bridegroom, who will be taken away by crucifixion, causing the disciples to mourn.

Jesus heals a bleeding woman, and a dead girl. Luke names Jairus, the ruler of the Capernaum synagogue (Luke 8:41), who fell at Jesus' feet and begged healing for his only child—a twelve-year old girl. Jairus offers a perfect formula for intercession—<u>come</u> to Jesus, <u>kneel</u>, and <u>beg</u>. Jairus knows his daughter is dead, but has faith that Jesus has the power to restore her life. Sandwiched in between the ruler's crisis is the plight of a hemorrhaging woman, who knows that if she can touch the hem of Jesus' garment, she can be healed. Although a bleeding woman touching an observant Jew will make him ritually unclean, the power of Jesus heals and cleanses the woman. Framing the story of the hemorrhaging woman, Matthew returns to the plight of Jairus. Professional mourners mock Jesus, when He says, *"Depart; for the girl is not dead but sleeping"* (Matthew 9:24). Jesus knows that death is not the last word. Jesus has power over life and death. Christians believe in the resurrection of the body. When Jesus comes in glory, He will re-unite our bodies and souls to live for all eternity. Jesus gives life to this dead girl.

Finally, Jesus restores sight to two blind men, and heals a mute, demon possessed man. Jesus fulfills the prophecies of Isaiah. The blind see, the mute speak, the dead are raised. The Pharisees could read; they knew the Old Testament prophecies. They could have helped people recognize the fulfillment of God's promises in Jesus. Instead, the Pharisees attribute the miracles of Jesus to the evil one. How could the Pharisees be so blind? The Pharisees are spiritually blind and refuse to acknowledge Jesus and His power. Bible knowledge is not enough. The demons recognize Jesus as the Son of God, but it does them no good. Just as Matthew responded to Jesus' invitation with joy, so we may follow Jesus with faith and joy.

Perhaps the Gospel writers want to place before us the depth of misery that Jesus was prepared to confront. Blindness, in His time, was considered as repulsive as leprosy. People were afraid to touch the blind. Very often, blindness was caused by some infection or disease—resulting in a grotesque redness or swollenness and a constant running of the eyes. . . . Moreover, the self-righteous leaders in the days of Jesus would have added to the misery of the blind by accusing them of being sinners whom God had punished. . . . In short: the blind were normally helpless, rejected, and discarded by society; and they could only survive through the mercy of others. . .

In today's Gospel [Matthew 9:27–31], Jesus doesn't just talk to the two blind men. He touches them at the point of their oppression in order to give back their human dignity. . . . Christian charity is first of all the simple response to immediate needs and specific situations: feeding the hungry, clothing the naked, caring for and healing the sick, visiting those in prison. How great has been the witness of the Church down the centuries in providing immediate and indiscriminate assistance to those in any kind of misery! . . .

But the most tragic of all poverties here is the rejection and exclusion of God from all social and economic life, the rebellion against divine laws written in human nature, with the aim of creating new laws and even a new global ethic on the levels of sexuality, family, life. . . . But, like Jesus, we cannot stop at the healing of the immediate need, be it physical or material. Yes, Jesus cures the sick, feeds the hungry, gives sight to the blind and makes the deaf hear. In this one chapter of Matthew, He heals a paralytic, restores a young girl to life, relieves a woman suffering from a hemorrhage and cures a mute demoniac. . .

In His healing actions, Jesus has come to bring the goodness of the Father who sends Him and, at the same time, leads the suffering to the joy of knowing the Lord, who frees mankind from every type of gloom and darkness, that is, evil and the Evil One. . . . The deepest blindness of man is not to know God; and salvation is illumination. Salvation begins with God's causing light to shine in darkness—very often through acts of charity. But, even if people are given all their materials needs, until God shines in their hearts, they cannot see. In the words of Pope Benedict XVI: "If we do not give God, we give too little."

Robert Cardinal Sarah, *Homily*, December 3, 2010

1. How does the leper address Jesus? What does this signify?

Matthew 8:1–2
CCC 448

2. What does Jesus tell the healed leper to do? What does this indicate?

Matthew 8:3–4
Leviticus 14:1–4
CCC 586

3. What does the centurion give to us? Matthew 8:8, CCC 1386

4. What can you learn from these passages?

Matthew 8:10
CCC 2610

5. Describe the drama in Matthew 8:14–17.

6. What do Jesus' healings teach us?

Isaiah 53:4
Matthew 8:17
CCC 517
CCC 1505

7. Jesus was poor. Describe the scope of poverty. Matthew 8:20; CCC 2444

8. Describe God's relationship with nature. Job 26:12

Job 26:12
Psalm 89:9
Psalm 107:23–32
Matthew 8:23–27

9. What do the demons say to Jesus? Matthew 8:29

* How do those who torment others sometimes feel sorry for themselves?

10. What two things does Jesus do for the paralytic? Matthew 9:1–7

11. The Pharisees accuse Jesus of what sins? Matthew 9:3, 11, 14

12. Jesus calls Matthew with what two words? Matthew 9:9

13. What does God want?

Hosea 6:6
Micah 6:8

* How can you do this practically?

14. What can you learn from these passages?

Matthew 9:13
CCC 589
CCC 2100

15. Explain the healing sandwiched in this drama.

Matthew 9:18–19	
Matthew 9:20–22	
Matthew 9:23–26	

16. What can you learn from these verses?

Matthew 9:27–30	
CCC 439	
CCC 2616	

17. What did the crowds say about Jesus? Matthew 9:33

18. Explain the illogic of the Pharisees. Matthew 9:34

* How do you respond when people blame God for the problems in the world?

19. Identify a condition of the people and an attribute of God in these verses.

Matthew 9:36
Numbers 27:17
Ezekiel 34:22–24
Zechariah 10:2b
John 10:11–15

20. What did Jesus ask us to do about laborers?

Matthew 9:38
CCC 2611

* How has God called you to labor for Him?

** What can you do to pray for and encourage religious vocations?

*** Have you ever invited a priest or seminarian over for dinner?

Chapter 9

Mission of the Twelve
Matthew 10

You received without pay, give without pay.
Take no gold, nor silver, nor copper in your belts.
Matthew 10:8–9

The word "apostle" in Greek *apostellein* means "one who is sent out," attaching the prefix *apo*— "outwards" to the stem *stellein* "to send." Jesus chose twelve men as His ambassadors to the ends of the earth, to lay the groundwork for the City of God. In the Book of Revelation, they will appear as the twelve foundations for the heavenly city itself, the New Jerusalem (Revelation 21:14).

Many sermons and books have characterized the apostles as a ragged band of semi-literate laborers. That picture, however, is very misleading. In rabbinic tradition, those who sought the position of rabbi first learned a manual trade and then started a family. Only at age thirty did the rabbinic work begin. Hence Saint Paul, who was highly schooled by the best teachers in Judaism, knew how to make tents for a living. So those young fishermen on the Sea of Galilee may very well have been on a trajectory towards becoming teachers in Israel even before Jesus came along. Two of them, including Andrew, the brother of Simon Peter, had been followers of John the Baptist before they became followers of Jesus.

One man who was not on the seminary track was Matthew, the tax collector. Rather, Matthew was on his way to becoming a rich collaborator with the Romans, and no rabbinic school would have accepted him. No doubt, Jesus may have been interested in Matthew's scribal skills, which would eventually enable him to document the life of Jesus and the history of this movement. Matthew was certainly literate, but four other apostles also wrote books of the New Testament—John, Peter, James, and Jude. It is hard to believe that they could neither read nor write, considering the literary merits of their compositions. John has a flair for understatement. Peter speaks with raw power. James delights in metaphors, and the little letter of Jude makes allusions to other works of Jewish literature. Did all of those abilities spring up only after Jesus called them?

Jesus had an advantage over all other people who tried to change the world—He could create ahead of time exactly the kind of people He needed. Saint Paul says as much: *Those whom he predestined he also called* (Romans 8:30), *And how are they to believe in him of whom they have never heard? And how are they to hear without a preacher? And how can men preach unless they are sent?* (Romans 10:14–15). So the apostolic sequence reveals predestination, a call by God, sending out, and then preaching.

THE TWELVE APOSTLES			
Matthew 10:2–4	**Mark 3:13–19**	**Luke 6:12–16**	**Acts 1:13**
SIMON PETER	**SIMON PETER**	**SIMON PETER**	**PETER**
Andrew	James	Andrew	John
James	John	James	James
John	Andrew	John	Andrew
Philip	Philip	Philip	Philip
Bartholomew	Bartholomew	Bartholomew	Thomas
Thomas	Matthew	Matthew	Bartholomew
Matthew	Thomas	Thomas	Matthew
James	James	James	James
Thaddaeus	Thaddaeus	Simon the Zealot	Simon
Simon	Simon	Judas son of James	Judas Son of James
Judas Iscariot	Judas Iscariot	Judas Iscariot	

And he called to him his twelve disciples and gave them authority over unclean spirits, to cast them out, and to heal every disease and every infirmity (Matthew 10:1). The first apostolic task is exorcism, before other forms of healing, before teaching. As long as people are in the grip of Satan, they will not be able to respond to the gospel. Moses led the people away from the false gods of Egypt before he taught them, from the mountaintop, about the true God. Jesus worked exorcisms and healed; then when even larger crowds gathered, He taught them the Sermon on the Mount. So on their first mission, the apostles are to promote the kingship of God and demote the reign of Satan by using the name of Jesus.

An unidentified man saw the apostles casting out demons in the name of Jesus, and he began to do so as well. The apostles tried to stop him, and John complained to Jesus. But, Jesus said, *"Do not forbid him; for he that is not against you is for you"* (Luke 9:50; Mark 9:38–41). The power belongs to the Name itself, and not to the one empowered by it. The apostles are training to become transparent instruments of grace to others, by a power that cannot be controlled or contained.

Simon, who is called Peter, and Andrew his brother; James the son of Zebedee, and John his brother (Matthew 10:2). This is definitely the core group, the inner circle of the twelve apostles. When Jesus travels with four apostles, they are these same two sets of brothers, called from their fishing boats in the Sea of Galilee (Matthew 4:18–22).

Whenever Jesus travels with three apostles, they are always Peter, James and John. These three climb Mount Tabor to experience the transfiguration (Matthew 17:1). Whenever Jesus travels with two apostles, they are always Peter and John. At the Last Supper, Peter and John sit closest to Jesus (John 13:23–24). Even after Pentecost, Peter and John keep going up to the temple together to pray at the ninth hour (Acts 3:1), heal a man crippled from birth (Acts 3:7), are arrested (Acts 4:1), and summoned together before the Sanhedrin (Acts 4:7).

Whenever Jesus takes one apostle apart by himself, it is always Peter. Peter leads this group of four, as well as the whole band of the twelve. There are four lists of apostles given in the New Testament (Matthew 10:2–4, Mark 3:13–19; Luke 6:12–16, and Acts 1:13), and the lists are not in the same order, but Peter is always first. The other three apostles switch places—Andrew goes back and forth between second and fourth place; James between second and third; John between third and fourth—but Peter always keeps the same position—first among the apostles.

Philip and Bartholomew; Thomas and Matthew the tax collector (Matthew 10:3a)— Philip always appears first in the second group of apostles, even though the others change positions within the group. After Jesus called Philip, he went to find Nathanael, so their friendship pre-dated their call as disciples (John 1:43–45). When Philip appears in the three synoptic gospels, he is always in the company of Bartholomew. An ancient tradition revelas that the man called in Hebrew *Nathana-El* "gift of God" is the same one called in Aramaic *Bar-Tholomew* "son of the plowman." Nathanael came from Cana in Galilee (John 21:2) and thus was surely present at the wedding feast of Cana, which Jesus attended with His disciples (John 2:2). Ancient tradition reports that both Thomas and Bartholomew went to India, where the latter left a copy of the Gospel of Matthew.

James the son of Alphaeus, and Thaddaeus; Simon the Cananaean, and Judas Iscariot, who betrayed him (Matthew 10:3b–4)—James son of Alphaeus leads the third group, because his name appears first in all four lists. This group contains as many as three relatives of the Lord. Later in this gospel, the residents of Nazareth name four relatives of Jesus as James, Joses, Judas, and Simon (Matthew 13:55); that matches the names in the third group of apostles. The relative named Judas there was not the apostle Judas Iscariot but probably Jude Thaddaeus.

These Twelve Jesus sent out (Matthew 10:5). Matthew has one sending, but Luke has two. In Luke, Jesus first sends out the twelve apostles (Luke 9:1–2) and later sends out the much larger group of seventy disciples two-by-two (Luke 10:1). There may have been even more training missions left unmentioned by the evangelists. The rest of Matthew 10 comprises a lengthy set of instructions, which the apostles received as they were sent out on their first missionary journey.

"Go rather to the lost sheep of the house of Israel. And preach as you go, saying, 'The kingdom of heaven is at hand'" (Matthew 10:6–7). Matthew had summarized the teaching of John the Baptist and Jesus with the words, *"Repent, for the kingdom of heaven is at hand"* (Matthew 3:2; 4:17). Now Jesus sends the apostles with instructions to preach,

"The kingdom of heaven is at hand" (Matthew 10:7). Clearly, the Master desires that the apostles preach in continuity with His own preaching and that of John the Baptist. They are not to build a kingdom for themselves, but to prepare citizens for membership in the kingdom of heaven.

"You received without pay, give without pay" (Matthew 10:8). This sentence reveals the interior logic of the mission journey. Jesus chose His disciples from the margins and brought them in to the center, but now He sends them back out to the margins of society again, entrusted with a task of evangelism. Many have been called, but some have been chosen to go give back in return. Every apostle has two vocations, first to follow, then to serve. Saint Augustine of Hippo expressed this double call on the anniversary of his ordination, "For you I am a bishop; with you I am a Christian." This saying has been circulating in various paraphrased forms, but the original Latin is: *Vobis . . . sum episcopus, vobiscum sum christianus* (Sermon 340).

Both of these are graces, being called and being sent, but the one presumes the other. A bishop has to be a Christian first! Baptism is the first of all the sacraments, and one cannot validly receive any other without being validly baptized. When Saint Ambrose of Milan was elected bishop, he was still a catechumen; consequently he had to be baptized, confirmed, ordained deacon and priest before he could be consecrated as a successor of the apostles.

"Take no gold, nor silver, nor copper in your belts, no bag for your journey, nor two tunics, nor sandals, nor a staff" (Matthew 10:9–10). The twelve were young men, so they did not need walking staffs. They were going on short mission journeys this time, and could travel light, without bag, change of clothes, or money. The question of sandals is more problematic. Both people and horses need sensible footwear for traveling the roads. Roman legions wore *caligæ*, military boots, so they could cover territory when they were on the march. Ordinary people wore heel-covers, called in Latin *calcei*, from *calx*, "heel." Perhaps the twelve went out on donkeys, and would not need sturdy travel shoes.

Saint Francis of Assisi, seeking to follow the evangelical counsel of poverty, introduced the custom of going barefoot. Discalced Franciscans, Augustinians, Carmelites and others at first wore no shoes, then adopted sandals in more demanding climates.

"Behold, I send you out as sheep in the midst of wolves; so be wise as serpents and innocent as doves" (Matthew 10:16). Three similes present themselves in a single verse; you must be like sheep, like serpents, and like doves. That sounds like a mixture of metaphors, but all three are animal images, and that gives them unity in the semantic field. Also Jesus is speaking of not one but several virtues needed by His missionary workers. They must be docile to the will of God, wise in the ways of the kingdom, and innocent of involvement in the ways of the world.

The Code of Canon Law forbids members of the clergy from engaging in retail trade or holding public office. These canons do not preclude selling religious articles in a church basement, or acting in an advisory capacity on government boards. However, members of the clergy are not to compete with lay people who need to make a living, and history is replete with bad consequences when clerics have taken the helms of state in Europe and Latin America. The clergy have their own proper roles to play in teaching and sanctification, so that the laity may be endowed with good values to bring into the public arena.

"Nothing is covered that will not be revealed, or hidden that will not be known" (Matthew 10:26). Here Jesus says things reminiscent of the Sermon on the Mount. Near the beginning of that address, appears a metaphor, *"You are the light of the world. A city set on a hill cannot be hidden. Nor do men light a lamp and put it under a bushel, but on a stand, and it gives light to all in the house. Let your light so shine before men, that they may see your good works and give glory to your Father who is in heaven"* (Matthew 5:14–16). Later comes a counterbalance, *"Do not give dogs what is holy; and do not throw your pearls before swine, lest they trample them under foot and turn to attack you"* (Matthew 7:6).

Jesus makes two counterbalancing remarks. On the one hand He says, *"What I tell you in the dark, utter in the light; and what you hear whispered, proclaim upon the housetops"* (Matthew 10:27). On the other hand He just said, *"When they persecute you in one town, flee to the next"* (Matthew 10:23). These remarks are not contradictory, because when the light shines, the light itself will reveal where the fault lines lie between the two kinds of recipients, eager or unwilling. Unless we shine light in the first place, we will leave everyone in darkness. Thus the church has to proclaim the message in season and out of season.

"Are not two sparrows sold for a penny? And not one of them will fall to the ground without your Father's will" (Matthew 10:29). This imagery recalls the Sermon on the Mount, *"Look at the birds of the air: they neither sow nor reap nor gather into barns, and yet your heavenly Father feeds them. Are you not of more value than they?"* (Matthew 6:26). Psalmists yearn to flee like a bird (Psalm 11:1), with wings like a dove (Psalm 55:6–7), and have their youth renewed like an eagle (Psalm 103:5). Sparrows used to take sanctuary in the temple of Jerusalem, and made their nests in the rafters above the altar of the Lord (Psalm 84:3).

"He who does not take his cross and follow me is not worthy of me" (Matthew 10:38). The word "cross" appears here for the first time in the New Testament, and it refers to the cross of the apostles, not to the Cross of Jesus. The word flows off our tongues today without any shock value, but for people in the first century it was like the word "guillotine" or "electric chair" today. Only later, after Jesus took up His own Cross, did the saying enter into the fullness of its meaning.

According to tradition, at least two of the apostles eventually were crucified like their Master. Saint Peter was crucified upside-down in the Circus of Nero on the Vatican Hill in Rome. The last thing he saw was the obelisk still standing in the Piazza di San Pietro. His brother, Saint Andrew was crucified on an X-shaped cross in the city of Patrai in Greece.

Saint Andrew's Cross became the banner of Scotland, was absorbed into the Union Jack, and also appeared in the Confederate battle flag.

"He who receives you receives me" (Matthew 10:40). Jesus conclude with a blessing for those who welcome the apostles, hear them and respond. When one of the apostles went to a city, or later to a country, they came *in persona Christi*, as His ambassadors and agents. Similarly today, wherever a bishop goes in his diocese, it is as if Christ Himself is appearing in person. The Pope is Vicar of Christ for the whole world, supreme pastor of the church, but the bishop is Christ's principal agent in each diocese, and the pastor is the bishop's delegate in each parish. Those who give them welcome give welcome to Christ.

1. What authority did Jesus give the twelve disciples? Matthew 10:1–2

2. What special gift did the apostles receive to do their work? CCC 1556

3. Explain some cautions about money and ministry.

Matthew 10:8–10
1 Timothy 5:18b
CCC 2121–2122

4. What is the mission of the apostles? Matthew 10:6–8, CCC 1509

5. Who did Jesus choose as His twelve apostles? Why? Who succeeds them?

Matthew 10:2–4
CCC 858
CCC 861

6. What is Jesus establishing?

CCC 764
CCC 765

7. Explain something about wisdom and innocence.

Matthew 10:16
Romans 16:19–20

8. What warnings does Jesus give?

Matthew 10:17–18
Matthew 10:21–23
Matthew 10:34–36

9. How will the apostles be equipped?

Matthew 10:19–20
John 16:7–13
CCC 728

* Share a time when the Holy Spirit gave you the right words to say.

10. What characteristic is necessary for all believers? Matthew 10:22

2 Timothy 2:11–12
James 1:12
CCC 161

11. Who should you fear? Why?

Psalm 2:11
Matthew 10:27–31
Hebrews 10:31

** Do you have any inordinate fears of the wrong things?

12. What does God expect believers to do?

Matthew 10:32–33
Revelation 2:2–3; 3:5
CCC 1816
CCC 2145

* Share about a time when you were able to share your faith with someone.

13. What kind of family conflicts can occur over faith?

Micah 7:6
Matthew 10:35–36

14. Explain the following difficult passage.

Matthew 10:37–38
CCC 2232

** Have you experienced any conflicts with family or friends over faith or morals?

15. How does one follow Christ?

Matthew 10:38–39
Matthew 16:24–25
CCC 1506

16. How did Saint Mother Teresa of Calcutta model Matthew 10:40?

17. How did the Galatians receive Saint Paul? Galatians 4:13–14

18. What does it mean to "take up one's cross and follow?" Matthew 10:38

19. What is a righteous man's reward?

Matthew 10:41
CCC 1821

20. Who are the "little ones" in Matthew 10:42?

* What practical thing could you do to support those who preach the gospel?

CHAPTER 10

John the Baptist
Matthew 11

Come to me, all who labor and are heavy laden, and I will give you rest.
Take my yoke upon you, and learn from me;
for I am gentle and lowly in heart,
and you will find rest for your souls.
For my yoke is easy, and my burden is light.
Matthew 11:28–30

Messengers of John the Baptist approach Jesus—No one knows how much time has elapsed, since John the Baptist preached in the wilderness, and appeared at the Jordan River (Matthew 3:13–17) for the Baptism of Jesus, and his imprisonment. John the Baptist may have been in prison for weeks or even months by this time. Disciples continue to visit John, manifesting a corporal work of mercy—to visit the imprisoned. These disciples may still look to John for spiritual direction, rather than going to Jesus, which illustrates a challenge for every charismatic religious leader. Does the leader draw attention to himself, or does he point to Christ? Do the disciples simply follow an inspiring leader, or do they seek to follow God?

John the Baptist provides an excellent example for ministry leaders. John hears the call of God. He comes onto the stage of history, does his job, and leaves. He preaches a message of repentance, and may expect Jesus to follow with stern announcements of judgment, as the prophet Malachi foretold. *But who can endure the day of his coming, and who can stand when he appears? For he is like a refiner's fire and like fullers' soap"* (Malachi 3:2). Instead, Jesus shows steadfast love and mercy to sinners, offering them forgiveness and an opportunity to repent and follow Him. This may have been confusing for John the Baptist and his followers.

Contemporary Christians may face a similar problem when others are called to different ministries, various apostolates, or service opportunities. Why do some people pray the rosary in the chapel, while others pray their rosaries in front of the abortion clinic? Why do some Christians visit the sick and others visit prisoners? Some outstanding people teach in Catholic schools, while others home school. God calls different people for diverse work and service at various times.

Orthodoxy without charity can become rigidity and push people away. Charity without truth becomes sentimentality, as Pope Benedict XVI warned. Jesus came first as a Suffering Servant, to offer mercy and forgiveness to sinners. Jesus will come again in glory with a winnowing fork, at the end of time, to judge all people. Jesus shows the perfect example of being all merciful and all just. Disciples aspire to be merciful and just, but only God perfects these attributes. Only God is perfect in mercy and justice. Disciples must be humble and discerning.

Now when John heard in prison about the deeds of the Christ, he sent word by his disciples and said to him, "Are you he who is to come, or shall we look for another?" (Matthew 11:2–3). Here, for the first time since the genealogy, Matthew uses the Greek word *Christos* for Christ—the Anointed One. The prophet Isaiah foretold the coming of the Anointed One: *the Lord has anointed me to bring good tidings to the afflicted; he has sent me to bind up the brokenhearted, to proclaim liberty to the captives, and the opening of the prison to those who are bound* (Isaiah 61:1). John may be gently reminding Jesus, that as the Christ, the Anointed One, Jesus has the power to free prisoners. Jesus has the power to release John from captivity, but why doesn't He do it? Has Jesus forgotten about John in prison? Is it God's perfect will for him to remain in bondage and suffer?

Perhaps John is discouraged in the prison darkness. Contemporary Christians can get discouraged too. Jesus, you have the power to heal. You can lift the darkness. You can rescue me from this mess. I am sick and tired of being sick, tired, and broke. Suffering gets old. Jesus, You are the Christ. Come rescue me, please!

Jesus seems to respond to John's plea by giving the disciples a riddle. He tells them to report to John the works that they see Jesus doing. The works of Jesus demonstrate who He is, fulfilling Old Testament prophecies of the Messiah. *"Behold, your God will come with vengeance, with the recompense of God, He will come and save you." Then the eyes of the blind shall be opened, and the ears of the deaf unstopped, then shall the lame man leap like a deer, and the tongue of the mute sing for joy* (Isaiah 35:4–6a). Later Isaiah says: *I have given you as a covenant to the people, a light to the nations, to open the eyes that are blind, to bring out the prisoners from the dungeon, from the prison those who sit in darkness* (Isaiah 42:6–7).

Jesus performed all of these healing miracles in front of all the people. Matthew records them in chapters eight and nine. Jesus directs John's disciples, *"Go and tell John what you hear and see: the blind receive their sight and the lame walk, lepers are cleansed and the deaf hear, and the dead are raised up, and the poor have good news preached to them"* (Matthew 11:4–5). But, Jesus stops short of saying anything about opening the prison doors. John the Baptist languishes in the dark prison dungeon. Jesus knows that both He and John will suffer and die violently. Even though they are both innocent, they have a similar destiny that they must each face.

Jesus praises John the Baptist. Six rhetorical questions and three positive assertions refer to this messenger of God. *A reed shaken by the wind* (Matthew 11:7) refers to a people-pleaser, someone who changes depending on how the wind blows. One might think of politicians who change stances based on what they think a particular group wants to hear, or people who live double lives—pious at church and revelers later. John the Baptist does not fit that mold. Jesus reveals that John is a prophet, but more than a prophet, because John *is Elijah who is to come* (Matthew 11:14). *"Behold, I will send you Elijah the prophet before the great and awesome day of the Lord comes"* (Malachi 4:5). John straddles the Old and New Testaments. Unlike the prophets of old, John the Baptist has the privilege of preparing the people, welcoming the Messiah, and introducing Jesus.

"Truly, I say to you, among those born of women there has arisen no one greater than John the Baptist, yet he who is least in the kingdom of heaven is greater than he" (Matthew 11:11). Jesus' statement is puzzling. He affirms that John is great in a natural sense, but true greatness comes to those who enter the *kingdom of heaven!* Thankfully, John the Baptist accomplishes both. Great in a human sense, John also chooses to enter into the kingdom of God, becoming great in a spiritual sense, as well. John the Baptist will suffer the violence of beheading, as so many saints and martyrs have endured violence through the ages, displaying great courage and holiness.

Dancing and mourning—*"We piped to you, and you did not dance; we wailed, and you did not mourn'"* (Matthew 11:17). John the Baptist brings a message of repentance, preparing people with fasting and conversion, but some will not accept his message and mourn for their sins. Jesus, the bridegroom of Israel, comes, with gladness and joy. Flute players announce the bridegroom at wedding feasts in Israel, inviting people to dance with delight. So, people reject both the severity of John the Baptist's repentance, and Jesus' joyous gift of love. They criticize John for fasting and disparage Jesus for feasting. Like spoiled, disagreeable children, this generation rejects the mourning of repentance as well as the joy of Christ's mercy. They will not enter the kingdom of God either way.

Woes to unrepentant cities—Jesus speaks words of judgment, using a literary device called *apostrophe*—a figure of speech in which someone absent, or something inanimate is addressed as if alive and able to reply. The prophets of Israel said *"Woe to you,"* when they were pronouncing God's judgment on unrepentant sinners (Micah 2:1, Habakkuk 2:9, 12, 15, 19). Jesus uses this same formula to upbraid unrepentant cities. People of Chorazin and Bethsaida, two cities north of the Sea of Galilee, within walking distance of Jesus' home in Capernaum could see Jesus' miracles, and hear His preaching. So, they bear greater guilt in failing to respond to Him. Jesus lived with Peter in Capernaum, which receives a rebuke reminiscent of one found in Isaiah: *"How you are cut down to the ground, you who laid the nations low! You said in your heart, 'I will ascend above the heights of the clouds, I will make myself like the Most High.' But you are brought down to Sheol to the depths of the Pit"* (Isaiah 14:12–15). Just as the rebellious angels refused to obey God and were punished, so the inhabitants of these unrepentant cities will be judged for their pride and rebellion. They refuse to humble themselves.

Jesus pronounces severe judgment on those who reject Him. *"But I tell you that it shall be more tolerable on the day of judgment for the land of Sodom than for you"* (Matthew 11:24). In the Old Testament, God punished the city of Sodom for its widespread, gross immorality, and homosexual sins. *Then the LORD rained on Sodom and Gomorrah brimstone and fire from the LORD out of heaven* (Genesis 19:24). Jesus pronounces a judgment of doom greater than the worst punishment imaginable. To reject Jesus and His incredible gift of salvation warrants severe judgment. Rejecting Jesus brings catastrophic consequences.

Jesus thanks God the Father. *"I thank you, Father, Lord of heaven and earth, that you have hidden these things from the wise and understanding and revealed them to infants"* (Matthew 11:25). The scribes and Pharisees had worldly wisdom and knowledge of the

Scriptures, but the unfolding of God's plan of salvation escapes them. Here "little ones" refers to Jesus' disciples. *And whoever gives to one of these <u>little ones</u> even a cup of cold water because he is <u>a disciple</u>, truly, I say to you, he shall not lose his reward"* (Matthew 10:42). People must be childlike—simple, humble, and trusting to accept salvation. *"Truly, I say to you, unless you turn and become like children, you will never enter the kingdom of heaven"* (Matthew 18:3). Are you humble and trusting to God?

The mutual, divine relationship between Jesus and God the Father emerges. *"All things have been delivered to me by my Father, and no one knows the Father except the Son and any one to whom the Son chooses to reveal him"* (Matthew 11:27). The Catholic Church believes that God the Father, Jesus Christ, and the Holy Spirit are three divine persons, equal in being. The truth of the Holy Trinity would be impossible for humans to discover, if Jesus had not revealed this mystery to His disciples who then passed it on to us. When Peter correctly identifies Jesus as the Christ, the Son of the Living God, Jesus explains that God the Father in heaven has revealed this truth to Peter (Matthew 16:16–17). Jesus' relationship to God the Father underscores His teaching authority and His ability to forgive sins.

Come to Jesus. *"Come to me, all who labor and are heavy laden, and I will give you rest. Take my yoke upon you, and learn from me; for I am gentle and lowly in heart, and you will find rest for your souls. For my yoke is easy, and my burden is light"* (Matthew 11:28–30). These verses can comfort anyone who has felt burdened by life. The rabbis spoke of the yoke of the Torah and the yoke of the kingdom. The Pharisees burdened people, adding many legalistic demands from their oral traditions. In contrast, Jesus' yoke is light—to love God and neighbor. Jesus helps shoulder our burdens.

Jesus speaks of Himself as wisdom personified. *Come to me, you who desire me [wisdom] . . . for my teaching is sweeter than honey* (Sirach 24:19, 20). God spoke to the prophet Jeremiah: *"ask for the ancient paths, where the good way is; and walk in it, and find rest for your souls"* (Jeremiah 6:16). Isaiah offered an invitation to the abundant life, when he said: *"Incline your ear, and come to me; hear, that your soul may live"* (Isaiah 55:3). Jesus fulfills all of the prophecies that were so familiar to the people who were waiting for the Messiah, waiting for someone to rescue them, heal them, forgive them, and give them rest.

Words are not enough, though. Talk is cheap. People want to see action. *"Yet wisdom is justified by her deeds"* (Matthew 11:19). Jesus teaches with authority. He forgives sins and calms storms. He casts out demons, cures diseases, and raises the dead. Jesus transforms lives. He touches people and lifts burdens. His wisdom and teaching surpass anything the people have ever heard or seen before. Jesus continues to work miracles. Jesus gives an invitation—*Come to me . . . and you will find rest for your souls* (Matthew 11:28ff). No one has a better offer to give. No one can promise more.

---

1. Who poses a question to Jesus? What do they ask? Matthew 11:1–3

2. What does Jesus' answer echo and fulfill? Matthew 11:4–5

Isaiah 35:5–6
Isaiah 61:1

3. What do these signs demonstrate?

CCC 548–549
ICCC 2443

4. What do these passages foretell?

Malachi 3:1–2
Malachi 4:1–6
Matthew 11:7–10

5. Explain Matthew 11:11 in your own words.

* Describe a noted contemporary person, who also has spiritual greatness.

6. What can you learn about John the Baptist?

Matthew 11:11–14
CCC 523
CCC 719

7. Explain Matthew 11:16–17 in your own words.

** Can you think of any people who are never happy, no matter what you do?

8. With whom does Jesus identify?

Proverbs 8:1–3; 9:1
Wisdom 7:22–25

*** List some ways you could grow in wisdom.

9. Find some warnings were given in the Old Testament.

Micah 2:1
Habakkuk 2:9, 12, 15

10. Find a comparable judgment that Jesus makes. Matthew 11:20–21

* Can you think of a contemporary warning that went unheeded?

11. What is Jesus announcing in Matthew 11:20–24? CCC 678

12. What happened to Sodom and why?

Genesis 18:20ff
Genesis 19:24–25

13. How severe is Jesus' judgment? Matthew 11:23–24

** What do you think the Final Judgment will be like?

14. What happens in Matthew 11:25–27?

15. What does this signify?

CCC 240
CCC 473
CCC 2603

16. What does Jesus offer those who seek Him? Matthew 11:28

17. What characteristic can you learn about Jesus? Matthew 11:29

Isaiah 29:19
Philippians 2:5–8

18. What does Jesus' yoke offer people?

Matthew 11:29
CCC 457–459

19. For what does the soul long? Matthew 11:29

Psalm 116:7
Hebrews 4:1–3

20. Describe the yoke and burden of the Lord? Matthew 11:30

Monthly Social Activity

This month, your small group will meet for coffee, tea, or a simple breakfast, lunch, or dessert in someone's home. Pray for this social event and for the host or hostess. Try, if at all possible, to attend.

Jesus said, "Come to me, all who labor and are heavy laden, and I will give you rest" (Matthew 11:28).

Reflect on this verse, and recall a time that you felt heavy laden and needed a rest. How did God provide rest for you?

Some examples:

 ❋ *I was working and going to school at night. I was so tired, I could barely continue. Then a friend invited me to take a weekend vacation.*

 ❋ *After our last child was born with some problems, I was totally exhausted. My mother-in-law came to help us. God love her.*

 ❋ *Caring for an elderly parent with dementia proved to be more than I could handle. My siblings came together and we devised and shared a workable plan, by God's grace.*

CHAPTER 11

Kingdom Parables
Matthew 12–13

*The kingdom of heaven is like leaven which a woman took
and hid in three measures of meal, till it was all leavened.*
Matthew 13:33

The high holydays of Judaism originated as harvest festivals, and coincided with the ripening of the grain fields—Passover for the spring wheat, Pentecost for the barley, and Tabernacles for the fall wheat. Tens of thousands of Jews passed along the roads at these times, on pilgrimage to Jerusalem. Especially on the journey home, pilgrims were likely to run short of provisions. The Torah provides that farmers should not strip the fields entirely, but should leave some gleanings for the poor to sustain themselves. With gratitude to the almsgiving farmers, and to God, the source of all blessings, the disciples of Jesus pluck some grain on their journey home. Others look on them with disapproval, however, because the day was a sabbath.

The sabbath, a major theme in the New Testament, appears for the first time here at the beginning of chapter twelve, nearly halfway through Matthew's Gospel. The Pharisees have drawn their battle lines, and Jesus is more than ready to engage them. He easily wins the first skirmish, drawing a connection between His men and David's men, and thus between Himself and David. As Lord of the sabbath, He claims the right to provide the definitive interpretation of the sabbath law.

All of this serves merely as a prelude to the real issue—whether or not Jesus should heal on the sabbath. The miracles of healing demonstrate the mercy of Jesus, but also the great power of Jesus, and strongly suggest His true identity. His healings took place sometimes in relative privacy, but more often in the synagogue, on the street, or out on the highways and byways, in full view of the general public. The sabbaths were teachable moments for so many people, and Jesus did not want to forsake these opportunities for people to see and appreciate His miracles. Seeing miracles increased faith even in the spectators. Jesus is Lord of the sabbath.

"What man of you, if he has one sheep and it falls into a pit on the sabbath, will not lay hold of it and lift it out?" (Matthew 12:11). An alternate version of this question appears in Luke, where a man's son or his ox has fallen into a well (Luke 14:5). The Torah says that your son and your ox shall rest, but not that they must remain trapped in a well. If animals die through neglect, then, they were killed by those who chose not to help them. We cannot keep the sabbath holy by refusing to save someone's life; that would be pitting the commandments against each other.

Luke reported a similar occasion when Jesus pointed out that every man, every day unties his ox or his donkey and takes it to the watering place (Luke 13:15); this is not an emergency, but a daily chore that must be done. John reports yet another exception, when the ritual duty of circumcision falls on a sabbath (John 7:22-23). If a mother labored to give birth to a child on a sabbath, then eight days later the rabbi must perform the circumcision, on the following sabbath.

The legal precedent becomes a kind of metaphor. The man with a withered hand is like a sheep or an ox or a son in the pit, where the requirements of mercy outweigh those of piety. Jesus develops the sheep metaphor into the full-blown Parable of the Good Shepherd (Matthew 18; Luke 15). Jesus describes Himself as the Good Shepherd and the Sheep gate (John 10). Finally, these animals return in the Parable of the Sheep and Goats (Matthew 25). These major parables grew from this tiny metaphor of a poor man's sheep that fell into a pit.

"Every kingdom divided against itself is laid waste" (Matthew 12:25). Jesus withdrew from combat, but privately healed the sick people who followed Him. At this interlude, the evangelist quotes the passage: *Behold my servant* (Isaiah 42:1–4). Soon, however, Jesus returns to the public arena and heals a demoniac, whereupon the Pharisees accuse Him of being a devil Himself. Then, He makes an apt comparison to a civil war. If devils cast out devils, their kingdom cannot stand, any more than when Romans cast out Romans. In fact, Romans had a series of civil conflicts in the previous century, Pompey versus Caesar, Antony versus Brutus, and Augustus versus Antony, leaving a swath of destruction all the way from Spain to Egypt. Devils do not fight devils, but people fight people.

"The tree is known by its fruit" (Matthew 12:33). Jesus then returns to plant imagery, which He already used so beautifully in the Sermon on the Mount. Trees frequently serve as metaphors in Hebrew poetry. The just man is portrayed as a tree planted by running streams (Psalm 1:3; Jeremiah 17:8), and an olive tree in the house of God (Psalm 52:8). The just man's children are like olive shoots (Psalm 128:3), for his wife is like a fruitful vine (Psalm 128:3). Several of Jesus' other parables also use trees as a reference point—a mustard tree (Matthew 13:31–32), a budding fig tree (Matthew 24:32–35), and a barren fig tree (Luke 13:6–9). Trees must bear good fruit and so must we.

"You brood of vipers!" (Matthew 12:34). Spoken first by John the Baptist (Matthew 3:7; Luke 3:7) and then by Jesus (Matthew 23:33), these words summon the image of a nest of young snakes, hissing malevolently and intertwining like a conspiracy of evil. The original must have been something like *dôr harâshîm,* "a generation of serpents." The viper metaphor becomes extrapolated over the course of the next nine verses. This generation of vipers (Matthew 12:34) is evil and adulterous (Matthew 12:39), comparing unfavorably to the age of Jonah (Matthew 12:40) or to that of the Queen of Sheba (Matthew 12:42). Therefore, He will give them no sign but that of Jonah, who was in the belly of the whale for three days and nights, as Jesus will be in the sepulcher for three days.

Behold, his mother and his brethren stood outside, asking to speak to him (Matthew 12:47, Mark 3:32, Luke 8:20). These brethren appear as James, Joses, Simon and Judas (Matthew 13:55) or as James, Judas, and Simon (Mark 6:2–3). For many contemporary Protestants, these verses pose confusion on the lifelong virginity of Mary. However, a different mother of the first two men, James and Joses, is revealed later in this gospel (Matthew 27:56). These two sons cannot be children of the Virgin Mary, and also the children of the other woman who is also named Mary.

The term "brethren" can mean spiritual brother, full brother, half brother, stepbrother, adopted brother, first cousin, second cousin, or even nephew. Abraham had a nephew named Lot, later called his brother (Genesis 14:12–14). The greatest biblical scholars of all time and all denominations—Gregory of Nyssa, Jerome, Augustine, Thomas Aquinas, Martin Luther, John Calvin, Huldrych Zwingli, and John Wesley, among others, believed that Mary was ever-virgin.

Sacred Scripture calls only Jesus *"the" son of Mary* (Mark 6:3), and calls Mary, and her only, the *mother of Jesus* (John 2:1). By researching all of the statements in Scripture and Tradition about who parented whom, one can assemble a coherent family tree of the extended Holy Family, distinguishing certain blood relatives of Mary from possible blood relatives of Joseph.

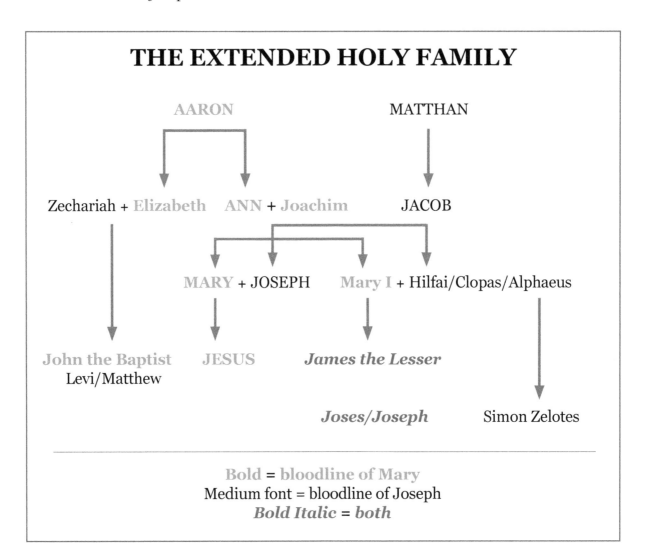

106

Luke and John provide a well-rounded picture of Mary's side of the family. Luke calls Mary a kinswoman of Elizabeth (Luke 1:36), who in turn is called a Daughter of Aaron (Luke 1:5); that means Mary and Elizabeth have a common female ancestor of the priestly tribe of Levi. John testifies that the Virgin Mary had a relative also named Mary (John 19:25). Their names might have differed slightly, one being *Miryam* (after the sister of Moses and Aaron, a very fitting name for a daughter of Aaron), the other in later Aramaic form *Maryam* (meaning "bitter is the sea," a name of sorrow). Tradition assigns to Mary's parents the names of Joachim and Ann.

Matthew calls Joseph's grandfather Mattan and his father *Jacob* (Matthew 1:15, 16; see Luke 3:23–24). The early Christian chronicler Hegesippus (AD 110–180), in the fifth book of his Memoirs, maintains that Joseph had a younger brother, whose name in Aramaic must have been *Hilfai*, which is transcribed into Greek two ways:

+ *Alphaeus* (initial H is dropped), the father of James the Lesser (Matthew 10:3; Mark 3:18, Luke 6:15; Acts 1:13); may or may not be the same person as Alphaeus, the father of Levi/Matthew (Mark 2:14).
+ *Clopas* (initial H becomes C), husband of "the other Mary," who stood at the foot of the Cross by her relative, the Virgin Mary (John 19:25). This other Mary is the mother of James the Lesser and Joseph (Matthew 27:56) or Joses (Mark 15:40). Clopas may or may not be the same as *Cleopas* (a Greek name), one of two disciples on the road to Emmaus (Luke 24:13–27), the father of Simon of Jerusalem in the Orthodox tradition.

These names are extremely rare, appearing nowhere else in Scripture. Four rabbinic figures had the name Hilfai, but they lived later, in the second and third centuries. Scholars debate whether Clopas is the same as Cleopas, and whether Alphaeus, father of James is also Alphaeus, father of Matthew, but there is no real data to distinguish them from each other. One thing seems quite certain: Clopas (John 19:25) and Alphaeus (Matthew 10:3) are married to the same woman. Alphaeus is the father of James (Matthew 10:3), who is the son of "the other Mary" (Matthew 27:56), who is the wife of Clopas (John 19:25). So Alphaeus and Clopas must be one and the same man.

Pieces of the family puzzle form an interesting picture when assembled. Two close relatives (Miryam and Maryam) seem to have married two brothers (Joseph and Hilfai). Their offspring, then, would be closer than cousins; they are double cousins. Thus Jesus on the one hand, and James and Joses on the other hand, would be legally and socially bonded as "brothers." Matthew knows that Jesus is not so related, because of the Virgin Birth that he himself described, but how many others knew at the time? The only people who knew for sure were Mary, Joseph, Elizabeth, and Zechariah. Did the sister know? Maybe. Did the cousins know? Unlikely. Did the neighbors know? Definitely not! They call Jesus "son of Joseph," and so He was for purposes of law and of heritage. To the same extent that Joseph is father to Jesus, James and Joses are double cousins, and thus they seem to be almost virtual brothers to Jesus.

And he told them many things in parables, saying: "A sower went out to sow" (Matthew 13:3). After the cameo appearance by His mother and brethren, Jesus takes to a boat and ratchets up His discourse by delivering parables. In the last chapter, He spoke in short metaphors but now develops much larger comparative tales. This first one is technically an allegory, since the word "like" is missing. After telling the tale, though, Jesus will make the several comparisons explicit.

METAPHOR short comparison without "like" You are a sower.	**ALLEGORY** longer tale without "like" A sower went out to sow.
SIMILE short comparison with "like" You are *like* a sower.	**PARABLE** longer tale with "like" You are *like* a sower who . . .

Matthew relates twenty-three parables in all (nine unique to his Gospel), compared to twenty-seven in Luke (fourteen unique), and nine in the short Gospel of Mark (only one unique). Eight of Matthew's parables, more than a third of his parables, appear in this chapter—the parables of the Sower, the Enemy, the Mustard Seed, the Leaven, the Hidden Treasure, the Pearl, the Net, and the Householder.

The first three parables are closely related and interlinked; all three of them have to do with agriculture. Many of the listeners were probably farmers themselves, and the urban people of the time were never very far removed from the fields. Jesus on the boat, and the people on the shore, could see fields and gardens around the rim of the Sea of Galilee, to the right and to the left of them. Jesus points to verdant nature itself as a visual aid, as He did in the Sermon on the Mount.

Jesus explained the Parable of the Sower immediately after delivering it, in Matthew and in Mark. Both accounts describe the kind of follow-up that Jesus no doubt gave after many or all of His parables. Some commentators believe that the parable proves that, in the arid countryside of the time, farmers spread seed first and plowed second. Perhaps they waited to make sure that rain fell, then put the seed on the ground as quickly as possible so that it could start to sprout, and then plowed it under for the plant to take root. The norm elsewhere is for the land to be tilled first, which lets the seed be put into the rows more precisely, with less waste of seed.

"The kingdom of heaven may be compared to a man who sowed good seed in his field" (Matthew 13:24). In the second agricultural parable, an enemy intervenes to try and destroy the crop by sowing weeds; the wise owner decides to let the weeds and the crops grow

together, and separated them at the harvest. Jesus gives an explanation of this parable too, but not immediately following. Two tiny parables intervene between this parable and the explanation. But, later Jesus explains the good soil as those who hear God's Word and live it.

John the Baptist and Jesus have used the term "kingdom of heaven" frequently in this Gospel, and now the phrase appears for the first time at the head of a parable. When a person thinks of parables, the words "the kingdom of heaven is like . . ." usually come to mind. Seven of the eight parables in this chapter begin this way, as do precisely half of the parables in this Gospel, thirteen out of twenty-three in all.

Three of Matthew's eleven kingdom parables occur also in Luke, where they begin instead with the words, *the kingdom of God is like . . .* (Luke 13:18, 13:20, 14:15). Many devout Jews of that time avoided pronouncing the title "God," so wherever they saw it written, they said "heaven" instead. Jesus refers obliquely to this practice in the Sermon on the Mount, when he says, *Do not swear at all, either by heaven, for it is the throne of God, or by the earth, for it is his footstool . . .* (Matthew 5:34–35). He observed this pious custom Himself when He taught His disciples how to pray, for He used the words "Father" and "heaven" but not the word "God" in the text of the Lord's Prayer.

Those avoiding the title "God" based this on the well-established practice of saying *Adonai* (Lord) instead of the Name *YHWH*. Only the High Priest could say the Name, and only while blessing the people on the Day of Atonement. Three times he spoke the Name, and three times the people prostrated themselves. Those in the temple, those outside in the city and the countryside, and those in far-away synagogues, lay prostrate at the time when they knew the high priest would be taking the Name upon his lips. The pronunciation came to an end when the temple was destroyed in AD 70, but prostration still continues in Orthodox and other synagogues, during the blessing ceremony on Yom Kippur.

"The kingdom of heaven is like a grain of mustard seed which a man took and sowed in his field" (Matthew 13:31). The second kingdom parable is one of the shortest. A mustard plant has one of the tiniest of seeds but it grows up to be *the greatest of shrubs and becomes a tree* (Matthew 13:32). The tallest variety of mustard is the *Brassica nigra*, or black mustard, which can grow to ten feet in height. The plant may have originated in ancient Egypt, and had diffused to the area of the Sea of Galilee many centuries before the time of Christ. The plant is an annual, and attains its height rapidly within a six-month growing season. So the parable is about how the kingdom of heaven will grow rapidly, once planted. Indeed, by the end of the first century, the Christian faith had become predominant in the Province of Asia.

"The kingdom of heaven is like leaven which a woman took and hid in three measures of meal, till it was all leavened" (Matthew 13:33). The first three parables were about men in their fields, and the fourth is about a woman in her kitchen. Women did work in the field, as Ruth did, particularly at harvest time when all hands were needed to gather crops before adverse weather destroyed them. Men did bake bread professionally also in ancient times. However, men did most of the fieldwork, and women took charge of domestic kitchens.

So Jesus provides images from both work environments. Again, this parable relates how rapidly the kingdom of heaven will grow, like leavened dough once it begins to rise.

"The kingdom of heaven is like treasure hidden in a field" (Matthew 13:44). Jesus leaves the crowds and withdraws into the house with His disciples, to whom He explains the parable of the enemy who sowed weeds. Since the apostles have returned to the field imagery, Jesus gives a fifth parable just for them, about hidden treasure. Recall His comment in the Sermon on the Mount, *"For where your treasure is, there will your heart be also"* (Matthew 6:21). Those who make the kingdom of heaven their treasure will know how to dig it up when necessary and display it for all to see.

"Again, the kingdom of heaven is like a merchant in search of fine pearls" (Matthew 13:45). Jesus continues giving parables privately to His disciples. The former tax collector, Matthew, is the only one who has saved this parable for posterity. At his booth, he examined pearls that were already harvested and in circulation, to assess their tax value. Pearls, like precious stones, were more durable than metals, and so held more stable value than gold or silver, bronze or copper.

"Again, the kingdom of heaven is like a net which was thrown into the sea" (Matthew 13:47). This maritime parable provides special interest to the former fishermen Peter and Andrew, James and John. When the fishermen brought in each morning's catch of fish from the Sea of Galilee, they had to separate it into three piles—kosher fish that Jews could eat, non-kosher seafood that only Gentiles could eat, and repellant sea life that no one would want on their table. Every morning, then, fishermen gave judgment on the seashore, as God will judge on the Last Day.

"Therefore every scribe who has been trained for the kingdom of heaven is like a householder" (Matthew 13:52). Jesus delivers this fourth small private parable maybe with an eye on the owner of the house, who is in charge of hospitality for Him and His band of close followers, serving the old wine first and the new wine later. Meanwhile, in the city, the crowds wonder at the wisdom of Jesus, and where it came from. They know His family, but they know nothing about His training. Rabbis then served periods of apprenticeship with already established teachers, and followed their methods. None of them knew who taught Jesus. Where did Jesus get such wisdom?

> There is no doubt that the parables constitute the heart of Jesus' preaching. While civilizations have come and gone, these stories continue to touch us anew with their freshness and their humanity. . . . We need to ask Him again and again what He wants to say to us in each of the parables.
>
> Pope Benedict XVI, *Jesus of Nazareth*, (NY: Doubleday, 2007), 183–184

1. What can you learn from these passages?

Deuteronomy 23:25
1 Samuel 21:1–6
Hosea 6:6
Matthew 12:1–5
CCC 2173

2. What is Jesus' relationship to the temple?

Matthew 12:6
CCC 590

3. Describe genuine sacrifice.

Hosea 6:6
Matthew 12:7–8
CCC 2100

* What type of sacrifice do you embrace?

4. What hierarchy of creatures does Jesus teach?

Matthew 12:9–12
CCC 342

5. List some characteristics of the Messiah.

Isaiah 42:1–4
Matthew 12:13–21
CCC 713

6. How will Satan's kingdom be defeated? Matthew 12:28, CCC 550

7. Explain some effects of repented and unrepentant sin.

Matthew 12:30–32
CCC 678
CCC 679

8. What causes eternal death? CCC 1874   How can this be avoided? CCC 1422

9. What can you learn from these passages?

Matthew 12:38–42
CCC 627
CCC 994

10. Describe the family of Jesus in the kingdom.

Matthew 12:46–50
CCC 764
CCC 2233

11. What passages could you cite to explain the perpetual virginity of Mary?

Matthew 1:24–25
2 Samuel 6:23
John 19:25–27
CCC 499–501

* Name some of the closest members of your home family and your church family.

12. Explain the parable of the sower. Matthew 13:1–9, 18–23

Seed on rocky ground
Seed among thorns
Seed sown on good soil

* Which of the above are you?

13. Why does Jesus speak in parables?

Matthew 13:10–13, 34–35
Psalm 78:2
CCC 546

14. Why do some people not understand nor accept God's call? Matthew 13:15

15. How blessed are people with faith?

Matthew 13:16–17
Hebrews 11:13
1 Peter 1:10–12

16. Explain the parable of the weeds. Matthew 13:36–43

17. Is hell real?

Matthew 13:41–42
CCC 1034–1035

18. What is the kingdom of heaven like?

Matthew 13:44
Matthew 13:45–46
Matthew 13:47–50
Matthew 13:52

19. What is the new treasure? Matthew 13:52; CCC 1117

20. Is Jesus the carpenter's son? Matthew 13:55

Matthew 1:20
CCC 495–497

Feeding the Hungry
Matthew 14–15

Then he ordered the crowds to sit down on the grass;
and taking the five loaves and the two fish he looked up to heaven,
and blessed, and broke and gave the loaves to the disciples,
and the disciples gave them to the crowds.
And they all ate and were satisfied.
And they took up twelve baskets full of the broken pieces left over.
Matthew 14:19–20

John the Baptist dies. As Jesus continues to work signs and wonders, word travels, and varied responses follow. One of the sons of Herod the Great, Herod Antipas, tetrarch (ruler of one fourth) of a small tract of land, fears that Jesus might be John the Baptist raised from the dead. Herod Antipas had entered into an incestuous marriage with his niece Herodias, who had been married to his half-brother, Herod Philip. Both Herod and Herodias divorced their respective spouses to satisfy their passions, violating Mosaic Law (Leviticus 18:16; 20:21). John the Baptist confronts this scandal directly. Herod fears John the Baptist, but Herodias hates him. Salome, the daughter of Herodias performs a seductive dance for Herod, and demands the head of John the Baptist on a platter.

Sick and infirm people flock around Jesus, wanting to be cured. Many people come just to hear Jesus speak. They walk long distances, sit all day in the hot sun, listening to Him preaching and teaching. At the end of the day, they are hot, tired, hungry, and thirsty, and Jesus has compassion on them.

You have heard the account of Jesus feeding five thousand men, plus women and children at Mass many times. You have probably also heard homilies suggesting that the real miracle involved Jesus inspiring the people to share their lunches! If that tired, old "Lunch Sharing" sermon is forever consigned to the trash barrel, it will be a huge blessing for believers! Where did such a crazy idea originate?

Since the beginning, faithful Christians have believed in the Bible as the inerrant, divinely inspired, Word of God. However, in the past few hundred years, some liberal theologians proposed a type of "feelings oriented" approach to religion, and sought to demythologize the Bible. Historical criticism attempted to verify the historicity of an event from the past, using historical science as the basis for evaluation. This method does not accept the inerrancy of the Bible as the Word of God, which would be unscientific and unhistorical. So, historical and scientific *theories* evaluate Biblical events. (Perhaps Jairus' daughter was just swooning. Maybe Lazarus was in a coma. Folks probably shared their lunches. Maybe Jesus only rose in the minds and hearts of His disciples.) Seriously?

Consider carefully the history and geography of the Holy Land in the time of Jesus. People in this hot, dry land have no refrigeration. There are no fast-food restaurants or obesity epidemics. Homemakers have no plastic wrap, aluminum foil, or sealed containers for leftovers. Bread quickly becomes stale. Meat is a rare treat for common people. If fish are not jumping, the family eats bread and vegetables, or nothing at all. Moreover, there are no printing presses, television or radio. No one advertises that Jesus will be speaking at the Capernaum Synagogue next Saturday, or by the seashore on Sunday. Nobody knows what Jesus will be doing next, or where He will be going, except God the Father, and He isn't advertising. No one has time to prepare. So, what *is* the actual historical context?

Word of mouth rules the day. Young boys run home and shout: "Dad, Jesus of Nazareth is passing by. Our chores are done. We're going to see Him." Mother might gather her baby and young children, and together with her husband join the growing crowd. Perhaps she has bread rising. She mixed flour and yeast, kneaded it, and let it rise. Later, she punched it down and formed the dough into loaves, covering it, to rise some more. But, she must not stop to bake it, or she will miss all the excitement. Perhaps she has a few olives or figs to bring along, or perhaps not. She may have nothing on hand.

Western people do not understand real hunger. In times of war or famine, people may go days without eating. Most contemporary people have never experienced days without food. But, in Jesus' time, hunger is reality. If crops fail, or drought or famine persists, people grow weak, faint, and emaciated. People die of starvation. Hunger reveals the true historical climate behind Jesus' miracles.

"The crowds represent all Israel gathered by Jesus. The baskets represent the 12 tribes under the 12 disciples. *Besides women and children:* Matthew's addition is very important, because the total figure could well come to 20 or 30 thousand; and it happens again (Matthew 15:38). Since the total Jewish population of Palestine at the time is estimated at half a million, Jesus is presented as feeding a tenth of the population."

Raymond Brown, et al, *The New Jerome Biblical Commentary*,
(New Jersey: Prentice Hall, 1990), 658

Imagine twenty or thirty thousand hot, thirsty, hungry men, women, and children. Think of a sports stadium filled with thousands of people. Now imagine that these people have not eaten all day. Think of growing teen-age boys, with their insatiable hunger. People have been sitting in the sweltering middle-eastern sun. They are sweaty, weary, parched, and famished. They have had no time to prepare food. Jesus arrives; the word travels quickly, and people follow. The disciples want Jesus to send the people away, so they can seek food in neighboring towns. But, Jesus teaches the apostles how to be good shepherds, to take the initiative, and to care for people's needs.

In the Old Testament, God also fed hungry people. During the Exodus from Egypt, He rained down manna and quail from heaven in the wilderness (Exodus 16:4–27). In a time of drought and famine, Elijah asked the widow of Zarephath for some bread and water. She gave him what she had, and he promised that her jug of oil and jar of flour would last until the drought ended (1 Kings 17:8–16). Elisha, the disciple of Elijah, did the same thing for a widow (2 Kings 4:1–7) and later fed one hundred men with twenty loaves (2 Kings 4:42ff). But the miracles of Jesus are so much more magnificent than anything ever before seen!

Jesus acts as a good host. He invites the people to recline, just as you might invite guests to sit down at table in your home. They have only five loaves and two fish for thousands of people. But, nothing is too small or insignificant when offered to God! Jesus takes the bread, <u>blesses</u>, <u>breaks</u>, and <u>gives</u> it to the disciples to feed the crowd. Jesus repeats this formula on several occasions.

. . . He looked up to heaven, and <u>blessed</u>, and <u>broke</u> and <u>gave</u> the loaves to the disciples, and the disciples gave them to the crowds (Matthew 14:19).	. . . and having <u>given thanks</u> he <u>broke</u> them and <u>gave</u> them to the disciples, and the disciples gave them to the crowds (Matthew 15:36).	. . . Jesus took bread, and <u>blessed</u>, and <u>broke</u> it, and <u>gave</u> it to the disciples and said, "Take, eat; this is my body" (Matthew 26:26).

The multiplication of the loaves and fish pre-figures the institution of the Blessed Sacrament at the Last Supper. The Eucharist anticipates the Marriage Supper of the Lamb in the New Jerusalem in heaven (Revelation 19:9). Just as Jesus gives the bread to the disciples to feed the crowd, Jesus authorizes the bishops and priests to confect the Eucharist for spiritually hungry people of all time, in all places.

Thousands of people ate and were satisfied, and there were baskets of food leftover. If you grew up in a large family, with many brothers and sisters, you probably did not see many leftovers. With five brothers in our family, we rarely heard the words, "Who wants this last potato?" When you feed adolescent boys, you know that it is almost impossible to fill up and satisfy them. Soon after leaving the dinner table, they may be looking for a snack. Baskets of leftover food in ancient Israel, is astonishing and miraculous. Jesus multiplied the loaves and fish. Does this miracle demonstrate the power of Jesus, the Miracle Worker, multiplying food, or does it suggest hungry people sharing food they don't have? Really? Think about it. Is God magnificently generous or do people share?

Jesus walks on water—Already, Jesus has shown His power over nature, when He calms the storm with a command (Matthew 8:23–27). Now, in the fourth watch of the night (between three and six o'clock in the morning) while the disciples are in their boat, being beaten and battered about by the waves, Jesus walks on the water to them. They are terrified and think they are seeing a ghost. Jesus says, *"Take heart, it is I; have no fear"* (Matthew 14:27). Here, Jesus' literal response is: *"I AM. Do not fear."* The response of Jesus echoes Old Testament references.

+ *God said to Moses, "I AM WHO I AM"* (Exodus 3:14).
+ *Fear not, for I am with you,*
    be not dismayed, for I am your God (Isaiah 41:10).
+ *I, I am he that comforts you; who are you that you are afraid* (Isaiah 51:12)?

Impulsive Peter wants to walk on the water with Jesus, and Jesus summons him. However, impulsive zeal combined with doubt causes Peter to fall. This will not be the last time that Peter's weak faith will cause him to fall. Fortunately, Peter knows what to do when he is sinking—he calls out to Jesus: *"Lord, save me"* (Matthew 14:30). Peter offers a good example and a perfect prayer to remember in time of need. Jesus rescues Peter. *And those in the boat worshiped him, saying, "Truly you are the Son of God"* (Matthew 14:33), providing the first of three declarations of faith in Jesus, the Son of God, in Matthew's Gospel. Both Peter, and the centurion at the foot of the Cross, make similar professions of faith later (Matthew 16:16; 27:54).

Scribes and Pharisees take offense. Religious leaders criticize Jesus' disciples for failing to perform ceremonial hand washing. According to the Torah, only the priests were required to wash before serving in the sanctuary (Exodus 30:17ff). But, the Pharisees took it upon themselves to impose this mandate on all the people. Jesus points out that they are more concerned with ritual hand washing than with caring for elderly parents. For the sake of their man-made traditions, they disobey the commandment of God. Jesus calls them "hypocrites," which they are. And, they are rightly offended. But, they do not back down. They refuse to reflect and repent. They have already made a decision in their hearts, concerning Jesus. They will not accept Him. They reject Jesus and need to get rid of Him.

A foreigner's faith—A Canaanite woman with a big problem cries out to Jesus. *"Have mercy on me, O Lord, Son of David; my daughter is severely possessed by a demon"* (Matthew 15:22). This foreigner humbly approaches Jesus, recognizing who He is and the power He holds. Jesus is silent, but she persists. The disciples want Jesus to send her away. Instead, Jesus explains His mission to reach out to the lost sheep of Israel. She persists. She comes to Jesus, kneels before Him and begs Him to help her. Jesus insults her and explains that it isn't right to throw the children's bread to the dogs. Still, she will not back down. She agrees with Jesus, and persists, reminding Him that even dogs eat the crumbs that fall from the master's table. A good master even takes care of his livestock and pets. The

Canaanite woman is asking Jesus to be *her* master and take care of her, and He does. *Then Jesus answered her, "O woman, great is your faith! Let it be done for you as you desire." And her daughter was healed instantly* (Matthew 15:28).

Jesus rankles Herod and Herodias, the scribes and Pharisees. Jesus heals the sick and demon-possessed. He multiplies loaves and fish to feed thousands of hungry people. He calms the sea and walks on water. Jesus heals the blind, the mute, lepers, and the lame. When people see this, they glorify the God of Israel. People continue to have various responses to Jesus today. Some, like the Pharisees want to get rid of Him. Jesus challenges our way of life, and cramps our style. There is no room for God in the public square. Others, seek Him, call out to Him, beg Him to save and deliver them and their loved ones. What response will you make to Jesus? Will you love and serve Jesus, or push Him away?

———————

1. Compare the requests of two women following banquets.

Esther 7:1–4
Matthew 14:6–12

2. What emotion does Jesus feel for the crowd? Matthew 14:13–14

3. Explain the problem and solution, which the disciples propose. Matthew 14:15

4. What does Jesus propose? Matthew 14:16

5. Jesus does what four things in Matthew 14:19b?

   . . . and taking the five loaves and two fish

6. Explain the significance of the miracle in Matthew 14:17–21.

Matthew 26:26–29
John 6:35, 51, 53, 58
CCC 1329, 1335

7. Where did Jesus go? Matthew 14:23

8. Explain the drama in Matthew 14:22–27

9. What does Peter do? Matthew 14:28–31

10. What does Peter's prayer indicate?

Matthew 14:30
CCC 447
CCC 449

* What titles do you use when you pray to Jesus?

11. What revelation did the disciples receive? What did they do? Matthew 14:32–33

12. What happens when people touch Jesus' clothes? Matthew 14:34–36

13. Explain the conflict between Jesus and the Pharisees.

Matthew 15:1–6
CCC 579
CCC 580

14. What does Jesus call the Pharisees, and why?

Matthew 15:7
Matthew 15:8
Matthew 15:13–14

15. What can come from the heart? Matthew 15:17–20

Galatians 5:19–21
CCC 2517
CCC 1853

* What is the condition of your heart?

16. Who is responsible for planting fruitful plants? Matthew 15:13

17. How does the Canaanite woman address Jesus?

Matthew 15:22, 25, 27
CCC 439

18. What does Jesus do for her and why? Matthew 15:28; CCC 2610

19. Explain the drama in Matthew 15:29–31.

20. Describe this miracle of multiplication.

Matthew 15:32–34
Matthew 15:35–36
Matthew 15:37–39

** What would you say to someone who insists that: "people shared their lunch"?

Simon Peter
Matthew 16–17

"You are Peter, and on this rock I will build my Church,
and the gates of Hades shall not prevail against it."
Matthew 16:18

When the Pharisees and Sadducees demand a sign from heaven, Jesus points toward signs that already appear there in nature: *"When it is evening, you say, 'It will be fair weather; for the sky is red'"* (Matthew 16:2). A red sunset meant desert sands were blowing from the east; a red sunrise indicated that maritime weather was coming from the west. On another occasion, Jesus reminded His crowd that a cloud in the west comes before the rain, while wind from the south brings heat (Luke 12:54–56). People can be good at reading the weather, but often get tied up in knots when trying to interpret signs from Scripture.

Jesus uses a simple metaphor, *"Beware of the leaven of the Pharisees"* (Matthew 16:6), but the apostles cannot seem to rise above a physical interpretation, even though they only recently heard the Parable of the Leaven (Matthew 13:33). Preconceived notions block the way to understanding for the Pharisees; literalism blocks the disciples. Jesus must be reaching a certain level of frustration at this point; any teacher would. By this point, some of the disciples should have learned something, so He asks a critical question, *"Who do men say that the Son of man is?"* (Matthew 16:13).

For some time, people had been speculating on who the coming Son of man would be. The disciples present a fair selection of candidates—one of the prophets of old like Jeremiah or Elijah, or a perhaps more recent figure like John the Baptist. They are thinking of Jesus, but they are not yet bold enough to start saying it. So then He delivers the clincher, *"But who do you say that I am?"* (Matthew 16:15).

"You are the Christ, the Son of the living God" (Matthew 16:16). Simon answers a direct question directly. Both for himself and for the other, more reticent apostles, he utters a profession of faith. John the Baptist proclaims: *"Behold, the Lamb of God!"* (John 1:36); Nathana-el says, *"Rabbi, you are the Son of God! You are the King of Israel"* (John 1:49). The Centurion cries, *"Truly this man was the son of God"* (Mark 15:39), and Thomas ultimately professes, *"My Lord and my God!"* (John 20:28). Those people all speak for themselves. However, Peter speaks for the whole college of apostles. Later, on the first Pentecost, five thousand will receive the Holy Spirit, but the one to deliver the sermon is Simon Peter (Acts 1:14ff). When Peter says, *"You are the Christ, the Son of the living God"* (Matthew 16:16), he begins to exercise the Petrine ministry, the definitive profession of faith in the name of the entire community. Peter's successors, the popes have continued to proclaim the fullness of truth in the Catholic Church for over 2,000 years.

Jesus asked about the identity of the Son of Man—a title of humanity, but Peter testifies that Jesus is the Son of God—a title of divinity. The first part of Peter's profession, *"You are the Christ,"* expresses his belief that his Teacher is the anointed one, translated from *Messiah* in Hebrew to *Christ* in Greek. The second part, *Son of the living God*, lifts the Christology higher. Jesus never actually uses the term "Son of God" to describe Himself, but others do, in His presence. When Jesus speaks of His relationship with the Father, the appropriateness of the accolade "Son of God" becomes clear. Offspring always share in the nature of their parents. Human parents beget human children, while canines produce puppies, fowl hatch chicks, and so forth. Jesus is unique, in that His Humanity coexists with His Divinity. He has two natures, not combined, mixed, compromised or changed, but retaining their unique characteristics while conjoined in a single Person. Many of the earliest testimonials combined a human title with a divine one, and in this way showed that they already held Jesus to be true God and true man.

Believer	Human Title for Jesus	Divine Title for Jesus
Peter	*Christ* (Messiah)	*Son of the living God*
Nathana-el	*King of Israel*	*Son of God*
Centurion	*This Man*	*Son of God*
Thomas	*My Lord* (Master)	*My God*

"You are Peter, and on this rock I will build my Church" (Matthew 16:18). In addition to his covenant name of Simon, Jesus gives him the mission name of "Rock." The original Aramaic was *Kephâ*, a boulder. The New Testament text transliterates the name as *Cephas* in a few places (John 1:42; 1 Corinthians 1:12, 3:22, 9:5, 15:5; Galatians 2:9), but usually renders it into the corresponding Greek term *Petros*, which becomes in Latin *Petrus*, and in modern tongues such various forms as *Pietro, Pedro, Petru, Peter, Piotr, Pyotr, Pietari, Piero, Pèir,* and *Pierre.*

Jesus' words are sometimes paraphrased to say, even in liturgical texts, "upon the rock of your faith I will build my church." To be precise, however, the Church is built not on faith in the abstract, but upon believing people. Peter himself understood what happened this way: Jesus himself is *that living stone, rejected by men but in God's sight chosen and precious,* so therefore *like living stones be yourselves built into a spiritual house* (1 Peter 2:4–5). That text is a theological reflection on the meaning of Peter's own name that he extends into an ecclesiology. The Church is an edifice of living stones. Yes, belief is what holds the house together. But, it is built out of real people, starting with Jesus as the head, then including Peter, and eventually incorporating the rest of us.

Jesus gives Peter the keys. The King of Israel always had a master steward in charge of the royal palace, as the keeper of the keys. Jesus as King appoints Peter as steward, to let people in and out of His palace, and to release the food and wine stored in its cellars. Peter and his successors are to be co-distributors of the graces that Jesus wins by his death on the Cross. Every Christmas and Easter, the Pope gives a blessing *urbi et orbi*, "to the city and to the world," to all people of good will. The keys of the kingdom are for our sanctification. The succession of Popes from Peter to the present day remains unbroken in the Catholic Church.

> Our Lord, whose commands we ought to fear and observe, says in the Gospel, by way of assigning the episcopal dignity and settling the plan of His Church: *"I say to you that you are Peter, and upon this rock I will build my Church . . ."* From that time the ordination of bishops and the plan of the Church flows on through the changes of times and successions; for the Church is founded upon the bishops, and every act of the Church is controlled by these.
>
> Saint Cyprian of Carthage (+AD 258), *Letter to the Lapsed*, 33

Jesus promises that *the gates of Hades shall not prevail* against His Church. This is a transliteration, since Hades is the word in the text. In the Gospels, Jesus uses the Greek term *Hades* interchangeably with the Aramaic term *Gehenna*, and the latter is probably the word He actually used. *Ge-Hinnom*, or the Valley of Hinnom, situated below the city of Jerusalem, was the place to dump trash. The smoldering fires became an image for hellfire. Also at Ge-Hinnom, besieging generals would station themselves to surround the city. David himself had done so, as later did Sheshonq from Egypt, Sennacherib from Assyria, Nebuchadnezzar from Babylon, and Pompey the Great from Rome. The valley represented a potential enemy base, and this contributed to its value as a metaphor for the forces of hell.

Some Bibles give the less precise translation *gates of death*. That rendering is actually a paraphrase, but the phrase *gates of death* does appear in the Hebrew Bible (Psalm 9:13, 107:18; Job 38:17), in contrast with the *gates of Daughter Zion* (Psalm 9:14, 87:2). Every day the inhabitants of Jerusalem saw corpses carried in funeral corteges out of the city through the gates of death, for burial outside the walls. These mournful processions were a constant reminder that human beings dwell in *the shadow of death* (Psalm 23:4, 44:19, 107:10, 14; Jeremiah 13:16). The two principal gates of death for the historical city of Jerusalem were:
+ Prison Gate (Nehemiah 12:39), from which dead prisoners were taken, and
+ Dung Gate (Nehemiah 2:13), from which corpses were taken to Ge-Hinnom.

"Get behind me, Satan!" (Matthew 16:23). Right after lifting Peter high, Jesus casts him low by calling him a Satan. What had Peter done? Because of his great love for Jesus, Peter simply tries to talk him out of sacrificing Himself to save the world. If Jesus took Peter's advice, then Peter himself would not be saved. The word *satan* here should really

not be capitalized in the biblical text. The word can be a proper noun indicating the Great Adversary, but it can also be a generic noun meaning one who tests or tempts another. Jesus surely means the word in the second sense, because Peter was motivated by love, while the devil knows only hatred.

"For what will it profit a man, if he gains the whole world and forfeits his life?" (Matthew 16:26). The Revised Standard rendering of the Greek word *psyche* as "life" here misses the mark. The word for life in Greek is *zoe*, not *psyche*. Jerome knew what he was doing when he used the word *anima*, and later translators gave the right sense, *"For what will it profit a man, if he gains the whole world but loses his own soul?"* The RSV sentence makes a weak argument, but the original version a noble one. Throughout history, the devils and their agents have offered to let people live, as long they are willing to give up their souls. What kind of life can a human being have, however, after making such a bargain? Many martyrs have given up their lives, as Jesus did, but kept a firm grip on their souls in the process.

Jesus took with him Peter and James and John his brother, and led them up a high mountain apart (Matthew 17:1). Jesus has gone up the mountains of temptation (Matthew 4:8), of preaching (Matthew 5:1), of prayer (Matthew 14:23), and of healing (Matthew 15:29), and now He goes up the mountain of transfiguration, called in tradition, Mount Tabor. The height identified today as such has a splendid view of the border region between Galilee and Samaria. In the Eastern tradition, mystical illumination is called Taboric Light. You can still climb Mount Tabor to this day.

Jesus takes along His three closest apostles, Peter and the brothers James and John. The number three is significant here, because these men will give witness to what they have seen on the mountaintop. In Judaic law, *"only on the evidence of two witnesses, or of three witnesses, shall a charge be sustained* (Deuteronomy 19:15, 2 Corinthians 13:1). One witness is insufficient to prove anything in a Mosaic court; two witnesses are sufficient, unless one of them is disqualified. The more witnesses the better, and three witnesses are ideal for establishing a cogent case.

And he was transfigured before them (Matthew 17:2). On Easter morning, Jesus will return in a glorified body, and on the Last Day, all the people who ever lived will return, and those bound for heaven will receive glorified bodies. Hence, the radiance in appearance and vesture on Mount Tabor was a foreshadowing of the Easter Body of Jesus and of the heavenly body of each of us. Many of the singular graces enjoyed by Jesus and Mary will be shared with everyone in the kingdom when the time comes.

And behold, there appeared to them Moses and Elijah, talking with him (Matthew 17:3). The mountaintop gets a bit crowded. Moses met God in a cloud on Mount Horeb; Elijah met God in a small breeze on Mount Carmel, and he also traveled to Mount Horeb. So these new figures are familiar with the mountains of the Holy Land. Now they have both added Mount Tabor to their itineraries.

Interestingly, burial sites for Moses nor Elijah were ever found. Moses appeared on Mount Nebo, another mountain, shortly before the Hebrews entered the Promised Land and then died. Elijah vanished into the skies in a fiery chariot. So far as anyone knew, they were both still alive, since there was no witness to testify to their deaths. The legend that Elijah would return before the end time was based upon this supposition. Elijah's name appears three times in this part of Matthew, once before, once during and once after the Transfiguration.

Luke adds the important detail that the two visitors themselves also appeared in glory (Luke 9:30–31). So the three chosen apostles are now facing a vision of three transfigured beings. The whole event is choreographed like a theatrical production, with an audience and a stage.

TRANSFIGURED BEINGS		
Moses	JESUS	Elijah
CHOSEN WITNESSES		
James	Peter	John

The Transfiguration reveals one of the important occasions when the three Persons of the Blessed Trinity appear together in the New Testament. God the Son is present in His transfigured human body. God the Father is present by means of his voice, saying, *"This is my beloved Son, with whom I am well pleased; listen to him"* (Matthew 17:5), the same words heard over the Jordan River when Jesus was baptized (Matthew 3:17). The Holy Spirit appeared as a dove at the Jordan River, but appears now as a cloud. So the three apostles are witnesses not just to the transfiguration of the three beings, but also to the three Persons of the Blessed Trinity.

"Tell no one the vision, until the Son of man is raised from the dead" (Matthew 17:9). Matthew and the other apostles were at the bottom of Mount Tabor, eagerly awaiting a report, but Jesus told Peter, James, and John not to share anything yet. After the Resurrection, four accounts of the Transfiguration emerge in the New Testament, in the Gospels of Matthew, Mark, and Luke, and in the Second Letter of Peter. The chief spokesman for the three witnesses is Peter himself, who many years later dictates this account: *For we did not follow cleverly devised myths when we made known to you the power and coming of our Lord Jesus Christ, but we were eyewitnesses of his majesty. For when he received honor and glory from God the Father and the voice was borne to him by the Majestic Glory, "This is my beloved Son, with whom I am well pleased," we heard this voice borne from heaven, for we were with him on the holy mountain. And we have the prophetic word made more sure. You will do well to pay attention to this as to a lamp shining in a dark place, until the day dawns and the morning star rises in your hearts* (2 Peter 1:16–19).

"Elijah has already come" (Matthew 17:12). This is the third mention of Elijah in Matthew 16—17. On the way down the mountain, the apostles are wondering if the vision they have just seen was the beginning of the end time, because Elijah has appeared. Jesus diverts their attention from the point of the question by mentioning that Elijah has already appeared in the person of John the Baptist, in the hill country of Judea. The land was already sanctified with people like Elijah walking through it, before the Incarnate Word ever set foot on it.

"Lord, have mercy on my son" (Matthew 17:15) sounds like the prayer of the father of the Prodigal Son (Luke 15:20–32). In this case, however, the son is an epileptic, whom the apostles had been unable to heal. The words *Lord have mercy* occur frequently in the Book of the Psalms, and also in the four Gospels. In the Psalms the word employed is the Divine Name, camouflaged by reading the Hebrew term *Adonay,* which is the basic term for a slaveholder or the general of an army. In the New Testament, the term *Kyrios* has a strong flavor of divinity, but still refers to the master of a household. Here, the father probably intends the latter.

"If you have faith as a grain of mustard seed, you will say to this mountain, 'Move from here to there,' and it will move" (Matthew 17:20). Again Jesus alludes to a parable that He has already told, when He said, *"The kingdom of heaven is like a grain of mustard seed"* (Matthew 13:31). At that time, He introduced the image; this time He gives the application. The quality of faith, like that of mercy, is not strained. A woman endowed with mercy has no streak of cruelty in her; a man endowed with the gift of faith has in him not a shred of doubt.

"Does your teacher not pay the tax" (Matthew 17:24)? Matthew is the only evangelist who mentions the temple tax, and since he was a tax collector it is not surprising that his gospel contains precise tax terminology. If Matthew the tax collector did not write this Gospel, then some other tax collector must have.

The temple tax was based on Old Testament legislation and Roman law. The Torah decreed that each registered male pay half a shekel, twenty *gerah* (Exodus 30:13). In the days of the Julio-Claudian emperors, taxation supported four religions—the pantheons of Olympus and of Egypt, Mother Goddess of Asia Minor, and the Hebrew God at Jerusalem. Everyone paid to one of these religions. Christianity was denied any standing as an approved religion, and in the year 67 the long centuries of martyrdom began. After the destruction of the temple in AD 70, Judaism was stricken from the list and the number of tax-supported religions was reduced to three. Both Christianity and Judaism thrived for the rest of the Roman era without state support, while the state-sponsored cults shrank into oblivion.

The term "Peter's pence" describes the annual support that bishops of the world send to help fund the ministry of the Vatican. The largest contributions are from the United States and Germany. As the result of the generosity of Catholics, the Pope is able to send diplomatic and charitable aid to nearly every country in the world. The so-called wealth of the church is located in the generous hearts of the members, many of whom give sacrificially, because they have faith in God and want to support the work of their church in fostering the kingdom.

> We also shall behold Christ, not as they then on the mount, but in far greater brightness. Not so shall He come hereafter. For whereas then, to spare His disciples, He uncovered only as much of His brightness as they were able to bear; hereafter He shall come in the very glory of the Father, not with Moses and Elijah only, but with the infinite host of the angels, with the archangels, with the cherubim, with those infinite tribes, not having a cloud over his head, but even heaven itself being folded up.
> Saint John Chrysostom (AD 347–407), *Homily 56 on Matthew*

1. How does Jesus respond to the demand for a sign? Matthew 16:1–4

2. What warning does Jesus give the disciples? Matthew 16:5–12

3. What enables Peter to make his profession of faith? Matthew 16:16

Matthew 16:17
CCC 153
CCC 424

4. What promise does Jesus give Peter? Matthew 16:18–19

5. Explain the importance of Saint Peter to the Church.

CCC 552
CCC 553
CCC 869–870

6. Explain the significance of the "keys of the kingdom." Matthew 16:19

Isaiah 22:22
Revelation 1:18
CCC 1444

7. What happens next?

Matthew 16:21–23
CCC 440
CCC 554

8. What must one do to follow Christ? Matthew 16:24–25

9. What is the scriptural meaning of the term "soul?" CCC 363

10. What does Jesus foretell?

Matthew 16:27	
Revelation 22:12	

11. Who went up the mountain with Jesus? Matthew 17:1

12. Explain the drama in Matthew 17:2–8.

13. What is the meaning of the Transfiguration?

CCC 554	
CCC 555	

14. Identify the Three Persons of the Blessed Trinity from these passages.

	Matthew 3:16–17	Matthew 17:2–8
God the Father		
Jesus the Son		
The Holy Spirit		

* What would you say to someone who says, "The Trinity is not in the Bible?"

15. Explain the coming of Elijah. Matthew 17:10–13

16. What does the man ask Jesus? What is his posture? Matthew 17:14–17

17. What did Jesus do for the boy? Matthew 17:18

18. Why couldn't the disciples help the boy? Matthew 17:19–20

19. What does Jesus foretell in Matthew 17:22–23?

20. How does Jesus handle the tax problem? Matthew 17:24–27

* Who is the current successor of Saint Peter? Do you pray for him?

** Explain the one, holy, catholic, and apostolic Church. CCC 866–869

CHAPTER 14

Servants and Sinners
Matthew 18

"Truly, I say to you, whatever you bind on earth shall be bound in heaven,
and whatever you loose on earth shall be loosed in heaven.
Again I say to you, if two of you agree on earth about anything they ask,
it will be done for them by my Father in heaven.
For where two or three are gathered in my name,
there am I in the midst of them."
Matthew 18:18–20

True Greatness—After Jesus establishes His Church and gives Peter the keys of the kingdom (Matthew 16:18–19), He gives a discourse on what community life should look like in His kingdom on earth. When Jesus teaches his disciples to pray, He invites everyone to call God *Our Father* (Matthew 6:9). If God is Father, all who enter the kingdom of God are His children—brothers and sisters in Christ. Therefore, all are *children* of one Father. The truly great Church leaders display humble service and mercy. Children in these passages can refer to little people, or to baby Christians—neophytes in the Church, who are just learning the ways of God.

Several practical directives for Church leaders and members emerge in the eighteenth chapter of Matthew's Gospel.

- ✦ Receive and serve others in humility (Matthew 18:1–5).
- ✦ Avoid scandal. Never tempt or lead another to sin (Matthew 18:6–7).
- ✦ Resist temptations to sin (Matthew 18:8–9).
- ✦ Seek out the lost and those who are straying (Matthew 18:10–14).
- ✦ Rebuke and correct serious sin (Matthew 18:15–20).
- ✦ Show mercy as God has shown mercy to you (Matthew 18:21–35).

Children, in antiquity and today, are vulnerable and dependent upon adults for their very existence. An infant or child must be fed, clothed, bathed, and diapered by an adult or he cannot survive. A little child cannot meet basic needs, or obtain food, but is totally dependent upon parents. Similarly, Christians are dependent upon God the Father for both material and spiritual existence and sustenance. Every breath you breathe, every beat of your heart comes from God, as long as He sees fit to allow natural life to continue. You cannot add one day to your life. You cannot save yourself or provide for your spiritual sustenance. God provides.

"Whoever receives one such child in my name receives me; but whoever causes one of these little ones who believe in me to sin, it would be better for him to have a great millstone fastened round his neck and to be drowned in the depth of the sea" (Matthew 18:5–6).

Previously, Jesus had cast the Gadarene demons into the sea (Matthew 8:32). A millstone, a huge stone, estimated at up to half a ton in weight, warns of a horrendous type of death, which is also alluded to in the Book of Revelation as a punishment for Babylon. *Then a mighty angel took up a stone like a great millstone and threw it into the sea, saying, "So shall Babylon the great city be thrown down with violence, and shall be found no more"* (Revelation 18:21).

Temptations—*"Woe to the world for temptations to sin! For it is necessary that temptations come, but woe to the man by whom the temptation comes!"* (Matthew 18:7). Why are temptations necessary? Because God created human beings with free will and the capacity to enter into moral struggles, temptations to sin emerge. Moral freedom involves the liberty to choose either virtue or vice. When one yields to temptation and falls into sin, inevitably it seems that he will entice others to join him in sin. In repenting of personal sin, the responsibility remains to help others extricate themselves from the enticements to sin, as well.

Sin and temptation are part of the human condition, and the result of free will. God does not cause temptation. *Let no one say when he is tempted, "I am tempted by God"; for God cannot be tempted with evil and he himself tempts no one; but each person is tempted when he is lured and enticed by his own desire* (James 1:13–14). Moreover, God does not allow anyone to be tempted beyond his means to overcome it. *No temptation has overtaken you that is not common to man. God is faithful, and he will not let you be tempted beyond your strength, but with the temptation will also provide the way of escape, that you may be able to endure it* (1 Corinthians 10:13). God's grace enables one to resist temptation. Prayer and frequent reception of the Sacraments help Christians endure.

Seeking the lost—God promised through the prophets that He would find and rescue the lost and those who have strayed. God Himself will be the Good Shepherd, who seeks out and saves the lost and forsaken souls.

- ✦ *He [the* Lord God*] will feed his flock like a shepherd, he will gather the lambs in his arms* (Isaiah 40:11).
- ✦ *"For thus says the* Lord God*: Behold, I, I myself will search for my sheep, and will seek them out. As a shepherd seeks out his flock when some of his sheep have been scattered abroad, so will I seek out my sheep; and I will rescue them"* (Ezekiel 34:11–12).
- ✦ *"My anger is hot against the shepherds, and I will punish the leaders; for the* Lord *of hosts cares for his flock* (Zechariah 10:3).

God wants to save the lost. He does not desire that anyone perish (Matthew 18:14), but Jesus talks a great deal about hell in Matthew's Gospel to warn people to repent and avoid eternal damnation. Heaven and hell are real. God does not *want* anyone to perish, but He allows it. Jesus uses hyperbole to express the importance of spiritual purity to enter the kingdom of God in heaven. *"And if your eye causes you to sin, pluck it out and throw it from you; it is better for you to enter life with one eye than with two eyes to be thrown into the hell of fire"* (Matthew 18:9).

> Jesus revealed to Saint Faustina the depth of His divine mercy as well as the reality of His justice and the torments of hell. **"Call upon My mercy on behalf of sinners; I desire their salvation. . . . O Blood and Water, which gushed forth from the Heart of Jesus as a fount of Mercy for us, I trust in You."**
>
> . . . "Today, I was led by an Angel to the chasms of hell. It is a place of great torture; how awesomely large and extensive it is! The kind of tortures I saw. . . . But I noticed one thing: that most of the souls there are those who disbelieved that there is a hell."
>
> Saint Maria Faustina Kowalska, *Divine Mercy in My Soul*,
> (Stockbridge, MA: Marian Press, 2011), 186, 187, 741

Guardian Angels—When you were a child, perhaps you learned a prayer to your guardian angel. Adults can pray this prayer too:

> Angel of God, my guardian dear, to whom God's love commits me here,
> ever this day, be at my side, to light, to guard, to rule, and guide. Amen.

"See that you do not despise one of these little ones; for I tell you that in heaven their angels always behold the face of my Father who is in heaven" (Matthew 18:10). Here "little ones" does not refer merely to little children, but to all disciples of Christ of any age, young or old. Traditionally, the Church has cited this verse as biblical evidence for the existence of guardian angels, who also appear in the Old Testament. *He will give his angels charge of you to guard you in all your ways* (Psalm 91:11). Each individual person has a celestial spirit assigned by God to watch over, guard, and guide him or her during this life. The Catholic Church celebrates the feast of the Guardian Angels on October 2nd each year.

Dealing with serious sin in the Church—Jesus delineates a three-step process for confronting believers in the community, who have fallen back into grave sin. The goal is to help restore a sinner to God's fellowship and grace, and to purge the community of wickedness. Ignoring or tolerating wrongdoing can plunge the community into depravity, and bring about God's wrath. The cycle of unrepentant sin and subsequent punishment unfolds repeatedly in the Old Testament. Tolerating unrepentant sin hurts the church and the society.

1) Confront the sinner privately in charity—*"If your brother sins against you, go and tell him his fault, between you and him alone. If he listens to you, you have gained your brother"* (Matthew 18:15). Motivated by love and concern, privately confront the sin, with the intention of winning a believer back. *"You shall not hate your brother in your heart, but you shall reason with your neighbor, lest you bear sin because of him"* (Leviticus 19:17).

2) Confront the sinner with one or two others—*"But if he does not listen, take one or two others along with you, that every word may be confirmed by the evidence of two or three witnesses"* (Matthew 18:16). This practice, originating in Mosaic Law (Deuteronomy 17:6; 19:15) attempts to convince the sinner of the seriousness of his or her wrongdoing, and bring repentance.

3) Tell it to the Church—*"If he refuses to listen to them, tell it to the Church"* (Matthew 18:17). Let the Church decide. Priests have been given the power to bind and to loose by Christ. Sometimes depravity becomes so grave, that the Church must excommunicate a member, or the entire community may fall into debauchery and lose favor with Almighty God. Unfortunately, history provides examples of wickedness going unchecked with grave results.

Mercy and forgiveness—Peter asserts his leadership and asks Jesus how often he should forgive a sinful brother, magnanimously offering to forgive seven times. Jesus' insistence on forgiving *"seventy times seven"* (Matthew 18:22) inverts Lamech's level of unforgiveness and vengeance in the Old Testament. *"If Cain is avenged sevenfold, truly Lamech seventy-sevenfold"* (Genesis 4:24). But, God is not like human beings. *How great is the mercy of the Lord, and his forgiveness for those who turn to him!* (Sirach 17:29). *Therefore the Lord is patient with them and pours out his mercy upon them. He sees and recognizes that their end will be evil; therefore he grants them forgiveness in abundance* (Sirach 18:11–12).

Jesus offers a parable to explain the importance of mercy and forgiveness. A servant owes the king ten thousand talents. Since a silver talent was worth over $1,000 this represents a huge debt to pay—$10,000,000. The servant falls on his knees and begs for patience, promising to pay back everything, which is, of course, impossible. The king, out of pity, forgives the debt! When a fellow servant owing a small amount asks for patience, the man, who had been forgiven, refuses to show mercy, and has his fellow man thrown into prison. When fellow servants see this iniquity, they report it to the king. The king then chastises the servant for not showing mercy as he had received mercy. The king then throws that unmerciful man into jail.

The moral of the story is that God expects us to emulate His divine mercy. We cannot expect mercy for ourselves, and demand justice for everyone else. Sometimes the evils committed are so egregious (rape, murder, betrayal), that it seems humanly impossible to forgive. In those instances, turn to the Holy Spirit, and acknowledge to God the inability to forgive. Beg God for His strength to forgive. God has the power to heal the wounded soul and infuse His divine mercy into a supplicant. Forgive your enemies and pray for those who persecute you. Pray and ask God for the grace to enable you to forgive.

Pray the Chaplet of Divine Mercy, and study the example of the saints, to help those who are unable to forgive to grow in mercy. Jesus forgave those who crucified Him (Luke 23:34). Many martyrs, beginning with Saint Stephen (Acts 7:5), forgave their executioners. Saint Maria Goretti forgave her assailant and prayed for his conversion. Saint John Paul II forgave his assailant. These examples can offer hope. Sin is evil and ugly. Mercy is divine, beautiful and healing.

When *[Saint]* John XXIII opened the Second Vatican Ecumenical Council, he said, "The Bride of Christ prefers to use the medicine of mercy rather than arm herself with the weapons of rigor." In his meditation "Thoughts on Death," the blessed Paul VI revealed the essence of his spiritual life in the synthesis proposed by Saint Augustine: poverty and mercy. "My poverty"—Pope Montini wrote—"the mercy of God. That I may at least honor who you are, God of infinite bounty, invoking, accepting, and celebrating your sweet mercy."

Saint John Paul II took the notion further with his encyclical *Dives in Misericordia*, in which he affirmed that the Church lives an authentic life when it professes and proclaims mercy, the most amazing attribute of the Creator and Redemptor, and when it leads humanity to the font of mercy. In addition, he instituted the festivity of Holy Mercy, endorsed the figure of Saint Faustina Kowalski, and focused on Jesus' words on mercy.

Pope Benedict XVI also spoke of this in his teachings: "Mercy is in reality the core of the Gospel message; it is the name of God himself, the face with which he revealed himself in the Old Testament and fully in Jesus Christ, incarnation of Creative and Redemptive Love. This love of mercy also illuminates the face of the Church, and is manifested through the Sacraments, in particular that of Reconciliation, as well as in works of charity, both of community and individuals. Everything that the Church says and does shows that God has mercy for man."

Etymologically, "mercy" derives from *misericordis,* which means opening one's heart to wretchedness. And immediately we go to the Lord: mercy is the divine attitude, which embraces, it is God's giving himself to us, accepting us, and bowing to forgive. Jesus said he came not for those who were good but for the sinners. He did not come for the healthy, who do not need a doctor, but for the sick. For this reason, we can say that mercy is God's identity card . . .

A Capuchin priest *[who spends many hours in the Confessional]* said . . . "I forgive a lot and sometimes I have doubts. I wonder if I have forgiven too much. . . . I go to our chapel and stand in front of the tabernacle and say to Jesus: 'Lord, forgive me if I have forgiven too much. But you're the one who gave me the bad example.'" I will never forget that. When a priest experiences giving mercy to himself like that, he can give it to others . . .

People are suffering. It is a huge responsibility to be a confessor. Confessors have before them the lost sheep that God loves so much; if we don't show them the love and mercy of God, we push them away and perhaps they will never come back. So embrace them and be compassionate, even if you can't absolve them. Give them a blessing anyway.

Pope Francis, *The Name of God is Mercy,*
(New York: Random House, 2016), 6–9, 12–13, 17–18

1. What can you learn from these verses?

Matthew 18:1–4
1 Peter 2:1–2
CCC 526
CCC 2785

2. Use a dictionary or the Catechism to define "sin."   CCC 1849, 1850

3. Identify the warning that Jesus gives.

Matthew 18:6–7
CCC 2284
CCC 2285

4. How important is it to eradicate temptations to sin? Matthew 18:8–9

* List some practical means you use to avoid near occasions of sin.

5. Does the Catholic Church expect you to take Matthew 18:8 literally?

6. What can you learn from the passages?

Matthew 18:10
CCC 329
CCC 336

* Do you pray to your Guardian Angel? Is this biblical?

7. Does God want anyone to be condemned?

Matthew 18:12–14
CCC 605
CCC 2822

8. Does this mean everyone will go to heaven? Matthew 18:9b, 34–35

9. What is your responsibility to someone who is in serious sin?

Matthew 18:15
Matthew 18:16
Matthew 18:17

10. Who has the power to forgive sins in Jesus' name?

Matthew 18:18
CCC 553
CCC 1444
CCC 1445

11. How can you obtain God's forgiveness? CCC 1446

* How often do you avail yourself of this opportunity? When was the last time?

12. Where is Christ present?

Matthew 18:19–20
CCC 1088
CCC 1373

** When and where do you feel closest to Christ?

13. Use a dictionary or the Catechism to define "forgiveness." CCC 277

14. How often must you forgive? Matthew 18:21–22

15. Explain the drama in Matthew 18:23–27.

16. How did the forgiven servant respond? Matthew 18:28–30

17. Who blew the whistle? Matthew 18:31

18. What was the ultimate outcome of that servant? Matthew 18:32–34

19. What does this parable teach about God?

Matthew 18:35
CCC 2843

20. How do Christians apply the parable above? CCC 2844

* What should someone do who finds it "impossible to forgive?"

CHAPTER 15

The Teaching Tour
Matthew 19–20

Let the children come to me, and do not hinder them;
for to such belongs the kingdom of heaven.
Matthew 19:14

Jesus travels into *Judea beyond the Jordan* (Matthew 19:1), an area east of the river inhabited mainly by Jews. Secular authors shortened this to *Perea*, or "the Land Beyond." After Herod the Great, his kingdom was split into administrative districts. The Roman military commander ruled over Judea and Samaria, though each community had autonomy in religious matters. Satellite areas to the north and east were formed into semi-independent city-states and small tributary kingdoms. Herod Antipas ruled over the two districts of Galilee and Perea, even though they were not contiguous. They sent him annual taxes so that he could maintain his lifestyle as he held court at his palace in Jerusalem, or in his stronghold fortresses like Machaerus, where he had imprisoned John the Baptist.

Jesus spent a large swath of His public ministry in the region across the Jordan, beginning with Matthew 19 and continuing into chapter 26. Although Jesus worked principally in Galilee and Jerusalem, Perea was the important third leg of His public ministry, for five likely important reasons:

+ Galileans, like Jesus, were fellow-subjects of the Pereans, under Herod Antipas (born about 20 BC—died after AD 39).

+ Jesus could expand His exposure to the sick, poor, and elderly Pereans, who could not travel to Jerusalem on pilgrimage.

+ Jesus could emphasize His royal heritage, because just to the south lay Moab, the homeland of King David's ancestor Ruth.

+ Jesus could stand on Mount Nebo and look across the Jordan to Jericho, just as Moses had done from the very same spot.

+ Jesus could identify Himself with His namesake Joshua, who had crossed into the Holy Land from the east bank of the Jordan, as Jesus would do (Matthew 20:17).

"Is it lawful to divorce one's wife for any cause?" (Matthew 19:3). Jesus had already addressed the question of divorce in the Sermon on the Mount (Matthew 5:31), but there were few people from *beyond the Jordan* there on that day (Matthew 4:25). This serious question may not resolve with a single reply, because marriage is God's plan, and divorce impacts families—men, women, children, grandparents, and society as a whole. Consequently, upon His arrival in Perea, someone asks about divorce and Jesus takes this occasion to deliver a fuller answer.

Jesus does not change His position, based on God's original intent and motivated by His mercy for the victims of social collapse. Divorce was not a theoretical question, but a pressing social issue. On the streets, Jesus saw women prostitutes battling hunger and poverty, after the death of a spouse or divorce. Ragged children were begging, some as orphans, but some abandoned by their fathers. Where was mercy then, but in the heart of Jesus, who refused to legitimize their suffering?

The problem of divorce and abandonment may have been greater among the Gentiles in the Decapolis (ten cities), since they lacked the moral training given by the Decalogue (Ten Commandments). Jesus had walked through the Decapolis en route from Galilee to Perea, and the sight of many street women and children was seared into His mind. So, He was of no mind to justify this great evil. God's original plan was the faithful marriage of one man and one woman for life. While it takes two to build a strong, stable marriage and family life, both or only one can decide to destroy it. Often, innocent people are victims of divorce, including children.

Jesus dignified marriage by elevating it to the rank of a sacrament, and also designated celibacy for a religious vocation. Herein lies no contradiction. Some who are called by God to the single or religious life may be pressured into weak marriages, because their parents want grandchildren, or people belittle them, thinking they cannot know happiness unless married. Jesus regards marriage as a source of holiness, and also wants people to respect those who seek sanctification in the single life, as all people do through the childhood years.

"Let the children come to me" (Matthew 19:14). Street urchins besiege the apostles, beg for money, and are brushed off, as so often happens to them. They beg Judas for coins, since he was in charge of distributing the funds for the poor. How horrified Judas must have been, seeing his petty funds shrinking! Meanwhile, Jesus remembers all the abandoned children He saw in the Gentile cities between Galilee and Perea, and His heart goes out to them. Jesus lets the children mob Him for love, while He lets them mob Judas for coinage. As the heart of Jesus turns to the priceless children, the heart of Judas turns away from true treasure to false. If only Judas could be like the little children, enthusiastically loving Jesus.

"Teacher, what good deed must I do, to have eternal life?" (Matthew 19:16). Immediately after Jesus welcomes the children, a young man musters the courage to approach Him. All three of the Synoptic Gospels report this. Luke calls him *a ruler* (Luke 18:18), more literally "someone who is from among the rulers." He was rich because he came from the ruling elite. Mark seizes the reader's attention with the detail that the man knelt before

Jesus (Mark 10:17). Matthew is the only source that specifically mentions that he was young (Matthew 19:20). Matthew may have identified personally with the rich young ruler, because he too had been challenged to leave behind a life of wealth. Tax collectors like Matthew did not belong to the elite class, but were allied with them and benefited from the system too.

First Jesus asks the young man about his moral foundation and addresses adultery first. In the Hebrew Bible idolatry was considered a form of adultery, a way of cheating on the heavenly Spouse. Adultery can lead to other sins as well. One who cheats in matrimony steals what rightly belongs only to the spouse, lies to spouse and children, dishonors parents, and fails to love neighbor or self. Young people need to practice purity to ensure their futures. Jesus said, *"Blessed are the pure in heart, for they shall see God"* (Matthew 5:8).

Satisfied that the young man has a good general ethic, Jesus invites him to the virtue of evangelical poverty. Anthony of Egypt heard *"Sell what you possess and give to the poor"* (Matthew 19:21), and went out to found Christian monasticism. First, however, he set up a trust fund to care for his sister, because he did not want to impoverish her in order to achieve perfection for himself. Monks and nuns are individually poor, but by living together in community they have had a tremendous impact on society. The Western world as we know it was practically created by religious orders during the Middle Ages.

"It is easier for a camel to go through the eye of a needle than for a rich man to enter the kingdom of God" (Matthew 19:24). This simple metaphor, presents a rich man like a camel with a load on his back. "Eye of the Needle" may have been the name for a narrow gate in Damascus or Jerusalem, through which camels could not pass. The text seems to involve a play-on-words, for the camel (*kamelos*) is like the word knot (*kamilos*) in Greek, and in the original Aramaic the two are homonyms, *gamla* serving for both. Matthew, who was fluent in both languages, did not make any mistake in rendering his gospel from Aramaic into Greek. When confronted by biblical humor, readers frequently start tying themselves up into knots.

The terms of the metaphor should not distract from the intended meaning. Affluence can be a problem and a burden. The apostles are unhappy to think that someone, who might have formed part of their band, instead went away sad. Jesus explains that this young man had much to give up, and therefore faced a big challenge. The kingdom was still open to him, but he would have to find an appropriate way to discharge his attachment to wealth that he was carrying.

"The kingdom of heaven is like a householder who went out early in the morning to hire laborers for his vineyard" (Matthew 20:1). Jesus makes a parable now about a rich farmer who dealt generously with his workers. He and the Twelve had encountered agricultural estates in the valleys of Perea. Flavius Josephus, writing at about the same time as Matthew, describes the terrain as "generally desert and rugged, and too wild for growing delicate fruits. In some parts, however, the soil is loamy and prolific, and trees of various kinds cover the plains; olive, vine and palm are mainly cultivated. These trees are also fairly

watered by mountain streams; and, if these fail in off-years of draught, then by steady springs" (*The Jewish War*, Book 3, Chapter 3).

Earlier Jesus told another parable about a householder, who has both new and old wine in his cellar (Matthew 13:52). This parable precedes the other, because wine has not yet aged, grapes have not yet been harvested, and laborers are needed for the vineyard. Jesus now defends the right of the owner to be generous with workers he has recently hired. The inhabitants of Perea and Galilee were often treated like second-class citizens, since those regions do not form part of Judea proper. Jesus assures the Pereans that they too have a place in the kingdom of God. Later people of every nation will find a place in the kingdom.

"Behold, we are going up to Jerusalem" (Matthew 20:18). Jesus and the Twelve now leave the country of Perea, go into the Dead Sea Valley, and up to Jerusalem in the country of Judea. From Mount Nebo to Jerusalem is only thirty miles. Nebo, however, stands 2680 feet above sea level; the mouth of the Jordan River 1365 feet below, and Jerusalem 3800 feet above. So travelers must descend 4045 feet and then ascend 5165 feet in the course of the journey. The changes of elevation total 9210 feet, and their feet will touch the lowest point on the exposed surface of the planet, with the heaviest atmospheric pressure. None of that would make for a very pleasant journey, with bandits camouflaged in the desert. Hence that very steep grade is nicknamed the *valley of the shadow of death* (Psalm 23:4).

No one could make such a journey in a single day, not even able-bodied young men in good physical condition. More likely they did most of their walking in the morning, resting in the heat of the afternoon under the palm trees of Jericho and bedding down for the night there, at the mid-point of their journey.

"Command that these two sons of mine may sit, one at your right hand and one at your left, in your kingdom" (Matthew 20:21). While Jesus was resting in Jericho, the mother of James and John approaches to request places of honor for her two sons, at the banquet in the kingdom. This seems like a strange place for her suddenly to appear, unless she had accompanied them all the way from Galilee. Her name, we learn elsewhere, is Mary, the probable half-sister of the Blessed Virgin Mary. She thinks it would be appropriate for Jesus to be enthroned, flanked by His two half-cousins, establishing a reign of relatives.

Jesus says that the two men will indeed drink from His cup, a promise fulfilled first in the Eucharist, and later in their martyrdoms. Then, He confronts the ten other indignant apostles. They were exhausted from walking, which may have affected their sour attitude. Jesus gives them instruction on leadership, and says that one must lead others by serving them. Better advice has never been given to any potential leaders, whether secular or ecclesiastical. Servant leadership is the model for the Christian life, as Jesus demonstrated.

And behold, two blind men sitting by the roadside (Matthew 20:30). The blind and poor often sit on a curb, interrupting the stride of the passersby and begging for alms. It is not common for beggars to sit side-by-side, unless they are family members collecting for their common needs. Perhaps these two blind men were brothers, cousins, or friends who joined together against the harsh realities of life. Perhaps one had partial sight, but the other none, so one could try to lead the other. Jesus had said of the Pharisees, *"They are blind guides. And if a blind man leads a blind man, both will fall into a pit"* (Matthew 15:14).

In the two parallel accounts, only a single blind man sits beside the road (Mark 10:46–52), and Luke names that man as Bartimaeus (Luke 18:35–43). So many details are identical that clearly all three accounts may describe but a single incident. The only difference is the number of blind beggars. How many were there, then, one or two? If Matthew remembers two beggars, he gets the benefit of the doubt, because he was an eyewitness, whereas Mark and Luke must rely on what others tell them. For that matter, there may have been several beggars, with only two shouting for Jesus, and only one of whom was named Bartimaeus. Naturally the one with a name stands out in the second-hand narratives.

Jericho was a priestly city, inhabited principally by members of the tribe of Levi, from the time of the conquest by Joshua. Hence, the priest and the Levite are going up from Jericho to Jerusalem in the Parable of the Good Samaritan; they reside in Jericho but go to the temple for priestly duties. Priests were on that road every day, going up in the morning, and coming back home in the evening. Thus it is very likely that the two blind men were beggar priests who could not perform priestly functions because of their handicap. If so, Jesus not only restored their sight, but also restored their ministry. The newly sighted followed Him at the end, because they too were bound for Jerusalem, to sing a priestly psalm or to offer a sacrifice of thanksgiving for the blessing of sight.

> "Let us listen to these blind men, who were better than many that see. For neither having a guide nor being able to see Him when come near to them, nevertheless they strove to come unto Him, and began to cry with a loud voice, and when rebuked for speaking, they cried the more. For such is the nature of an enduring soul, by the very things that hinder, it is borne up. . . . Not poverty, not blindness, not their being unheard, not their being rebuked by the multitude, not anything else, impeded their exceeding earnestness. Such is the nature of a fervent and toiling soul."
> Saint John Chrysostom (AD 344–407) *Homily 66 on Matthew*

1. Where was Jesus going? Matthew 19:1–2

2. What can you learn about marriage?

Genesis 1:27; 2:23–24
Matthew 19:4–6
Ephesians 5:31–32
CCC 1605

3. Why is divorce a problem?

Matthew 19:6–9
CCC 1614
CCC 2382
CCC 2386

* Share ways that Christians could minister to the divorced and children of divorce.

4. What do the disciples propose? Matthew 19:10

5. Explain the gift of celibacy for the kingdom.

Matthew 19:11–12
1 Corinthians 7:7–8
CCC 1579
CCC 1619–1620

6. How does Jesus feel about children? Matthew 19:13–15

* How does contemporary culture feel about children?

** Share some ways in which the Church reaches out to families and children.

7. What does the rich young man ask Jesus? Matthew 19:16

8. How does Jesus respond to the rich young man?

Matthew 19:17–19
CCC 2052

9. What does the Old Testament require?

Leviticus 18:5
Leviticus 19:18

10. Then what did the young man state, and ask of Jesus? Matthew 19:20

* Of the two men in this dialogue, who really kept all the commandments perfectly?

11. How did Jesus up the ante?

Matthew 19:21
CCC 2053

12. How did the rich young man respond to Jesus' suggestion? Matthew 19:22

13. Explain "detachment." CCC 226

* Do you have any inordinate attachments to things other than God?

14. What can you learn about wealth, and what does Jesus caution about wealth?

Wisdom 7:7–8
Sirach 5:1
Matthew 6:21
Matthew 19:23–24

15. What encouragement and promise does Jesus give?

Matthew 19:26
Matthew 19:28–30

** What would be the most difficult thing for you to give up to follow Jesus?

16. Find the moral of the parable of the laborers in the vineyard. Matthew 20:1–16

17. What does Jesus tell the Twelve? Matthew 20:17–19

18. Explain the drama in Matthew 20:20–24.

19. What does Jesus explain?

Matthew 20:25–28
CCC 605
CCC 2235

20. Describe the miracle in Matthew 20:29–34.

* How would you answer, if Jesus asked: "What do you want me to do for you?"

CHAPTER 16

Entry into Jerusalem
Matthew 21

And the crowds that went before him and that followed him shouted,
"Hosanna to the Son of David!
Blessed is he who comes in the name of the Lord!
Hosanna in the highest!"
Matthew 21:9

Jesus enters Jerusalem in triumph. Catholics remember and celebrate Christ's joyous entry into Jerusalem every Palm Sunday. Priests bless and distribute palm branches to the faithful. In some parishes, children re-enact the triumphal entry by waving their palm branches and singing, as they accompany the priest in the procession to the altar. This festive activity inaugurates Holy Week. Palm Sunday Mass culminates in the solemn reading of the Passion of Christ.

Throughout the Gospel of Matthew, people have been wondering and hoping that Jesus is the Messiah. Up to this point, Jesus has not given a direct, explicit answer. Now Jesus performs an action that reveals, beyond a shadow of a doubt, that He is the Messiah, the King of Israel. Matthew conflates two Old Testament prophecies to demonstrate that Jesus fulfills prophecy here. *"Behold, your salvation comes; behold, his reward is with him, and his recompense before him"* (Isaiah 62:11). *Rejoice greatly, O daughter of Zion! Shout aloud, O daughter of Jerusalem! Behold, your king comes to you, triumphant and victorious is he, humble and riding on a donkey, on a colt the foal of a donkey* (Zechariah 9:9).

Military kings came with horses, chariots, and weapons, prepared for battle and conquest. Jesus comes, meek and humble, on a beast of burden, as the Prince of Peace, the King of Kings. The zealots, seeking a revolutionary leader to overthrow the Romans, see clearly the peaceful kingdom Jesus brings. Jewish pilgrims approach the Holy City on foot, but Jesus comes riding on a donkey, the first time in the Gospels that Jesus mounts an animal. Usually, Jesus travels on foot.

Pilgrims re-enact some of the festive rites of the feast of Booths, by cutting down branches. After the Maccabees had purified the sanctuary and re-dedicated the Temple in 165 BC, the people cut down branches, rejoiced, and celebrated, even though the harvest time for the feast of Booths had passed (2 Maccabees 10:1–8). People spread their cloaks on the road before King Jesus, just as people had previously laid their garments before the king Jehu (2 Kings 9:13). The scribes and Pharisees know the prophecies well, see all this, and are appalled.

People shout: *"Hosanna to the Son of David! Blessed is he who comes in the name of the Lord! Hosanna in the highest!"* (Matthew 21:9). *Hosanna*, the Greek transliteration of a

Hebrew word means, "Help (or save), I pray." It is reminiscent of a Psalm. *Save us, we beg you, O LORD!* (Psalm 118:25). Catholics recall these passages, and sing the *Sanctus,* or "Holy, Holy, Holy" in the Holy Sacrifice of the Mass, just prior to the Consecration and reception of the Blessed Sacrament.

Jesus the just judge—Following Jesus' triumphal entry, He will perform two prophetic actions of judgment on the corrupt leaders in Jerusalem, particularly the priests. Prophets foretold God's anger and wrath against wicked leaders. *My anger is hot against the shepherds, and I will punish the leaders* (Zechariah 10:3). Jesus cleanses the Temple and then withers an unproductive fig tree.

Artists usually portray Jesus meek and mild, consistent with the Gospels. However, on this occasion, Jesus shows righteous indignation and reacts with anger and fury. The temple in Jerusalem was designed as a place for prayer, worship, teaching, and sacrifice. *Every one who keeps the sabbath, and does not profane it, and holds fast my covenant—these I will bring to my holy mountain, and make them joyful in my house of prayer; their burnt offerings and their sacrifices will be accepted on my altar; for my house shall be called a house of prayer* (Isaiah 56:6–7).

Priests approved and slaughtered yearling lambs without blemish for Passover, and animals or birds for sacrifice. People exchanged their money in the temple and then bought a lamb or pigeon to sacrifice. The priesthood had a monopoly, and prices inflated. The sacrificial system evolved into a corrupt business scheme that brought wealth to the priests and moneychangers, at the expense of the poor. Rightly disgusted at the sheer commercialism and exploitation in the temple, Jesus overturns the money tables and drives out the merchants, who were selling animals and changing money. Imagine the outrage of the men being thrown out of *their* place of business, and the priests observing Jesus making a mess in *their* Temple! But the Temple should be a house of reverence and prayer to God.

The blind and the lame come into the Temple and Jesus heals them. The chief priests and scribes see with their own eyes the wonderful miracles that Jesus performs. They could have repented and converted, but they are indignant. The Pharisees and chief priests see the prophecies being fulfilled, but are adamant. Children and simple people praise Jesus, but the learned elders refuse to see.

Jesus performs a second action of judgment, on a barren fig tree. Jesus hungers for righteousness and fruitfulness in people. He sees a fig tree, which should provide the sweetest of Levantine fruits. The tree symbolizes life. The fig symbolizes blessedness or beatitude. The fig tree and fruit are also symbols of God's people and the fruitfulness God expects. Because the fig tree has leaves it has life, but it has no fruit. *There is no cluster to eat; no first-ripe fig which my soul desires* (Micah 7:1b). Jesus curses the fig tree and it withers! The withered fig tree pre-figures God's wrath. *All their host shall fall, as leaves fall from the vine, like leaves falling from the fig tree* (Isaiah 34:4). The disciples marvel at the sudden withering of the fig tree, and want to know how and why Jesus did that.

Jesus responds with an encouragement to have faith, never doubt, and to persevere in prayer. *"And whatever you ask in prayer, you will receive, if you have faith"* (Matthew 21:22). Faith leads to prayer, which is an expression of faith. God always answers prayer, but not always in the way one expects. People often pray for physical healing. If disease persists, well-meaning Christians may accuse the sufferer of lacking faith, which promotes circular reasoning. God can cure illness. If uncured, do you lack faith? While perseverance in prayer pleases God, sometimes He has a different plan than temporary physical healing. All people will ultimately die. Full healing will take place in the next world. So, Christians pray in faith, trusting that God will provide what is best for each in His perfect timing.

Questioning the authority of Jesus—Jesus is not a Levitical priest. He is not the protégé of a famous rabbi. He comes into the city riding on a donkey, with people praising Him, throwing their cloaks on the ground before Him, and waving palm branches. What is going on here? Where are His credentials? Who gave Jesus permission to come into *our* Temple, throw over the tables, and heal the sick? The chief priests and elders demand to know *by what authority* Jesus ministers. They are the authorities in the temple, and they demand an answer.

Jesus responds in true rabbinic fashion—answering their question with a counter-question. If they answer Jesus' question, then He will answer theirs. Here comes a trick question. *"The baptism of John, where was it from? From heaven or from men?"* (Matthew 21:25). The chief priests and elders are wedged between a rock and a hard place, and they know it. John the Baptist was a Levite, but he didn't act like these Levitical priests. He lived in the wilderness, eating locusts and honey. John the Baptist preached repentance. People loved him and followed him. If the elders acknowledge that John the Baptist's authority is from heaven, they will have to justify their resistance to accepting and believing him. But, they cannot say that he is only from men, because the people recognize that John the Baptist is a prophet. They hedge. They cannot answer, and Jesus responds in kind with silence.

Following these prophetic actions of judgment, Jesus gives three parables of judgment on the religious leaders of Israel. The scribes and Pharisees in Jerusalem, who reject Jesus the Messiah, are depicted as:
  + A son, who promises obedience, but fails to obey (Matthew 21:28–32).
  + Wicked tenants who kill a landowner's beloved son (Matthew 21:33–41).
  + Builders who reject the cornerstone (Matthew 21:42).

Parable of two brothers—Brothers appear frequently in the Bible, from Cain and Abel (Genesis 4:1–10), Esau and Jacob (Genesis 25:22–34), Joseph and Benjamin (Genesis 30:23–24; 35:18), Ephraim and Manasseh (Genesis 41:51–52), to Peter and Andrew (Matthew 4:18), James and John (Matthew 4:21). Jesus tells parables about brothers as well, the most memorable is the Parable of the Prodigal Son (Luke 15:11ff). In Matthew 21:28–32, a father asks his two sons to work in his vineyard. The first son refuses, but later repents and obeys his father. The second son promises to obey, but does not follow through with his actions. The moral of the story is that actions speak louder than words. A confession of faith, giving lip service only, without corresponding faith-filled behavior will not be pleasing to God. It is not enough to simply "say" you believe in God. You must act!

Tax collectors and harlots were the most despised of serious sinners. For Jesus to proclaim that they would come into the kingdom of God before the elders of the people shocks and offends the priests and elders. While tax collectors and prostitutes are obvious sinners, many of them repented deeply and followed Jesus. The religious leaders, however, refuse to heed John the Baptist's message of repentance, and pursue the way of righteousness. Those serious sinners who repent represent the first son. God shows mercy to those who repent. Representing the second son are those religious leaders, who consider themselves already righteous and in no need of mercy, who stubbornly refuse to accept God's gift of salvation.

The parable of the vineyard—A Song of the Vineyard appears in Isaiah 5:1–7, and Jesus uses this imagery from the Prophet Isaiah to rebuke the religious leaders. The people recognize the references and Jesus' own message of judgment on the chief priests and elders. Below are some keys to understand the parable.

Householder — God the Father

Vineyard — Israel

Hedge — Commandments

Tenants — Religious Leaders

Servants — Prophets

Son — Jesus

Jesus knows that the chief priests and elders are conspiring to kill Him. The scribes and Pharisees *know that Jesus knows* they are conspiring to kill Him. Jesus has predicted His Passion, death, and Resurrection on several occasions in their hearing. But the chief priests and elders do not know what will happen to them. What will happen to the wicked tenants? *"He will put those wretches to a miserable death, and lease the vineyard to other tenants who will give him the fruits in their season"* (Matthew 21:41). Jesus knows and weeps over the destruction of Jerusalem that will occur in AD 70. Some of these elders may be among the one million Jews, who the historian Josephus says died in the siege of Jerusalem. In forty years, the Temple will be destroyed. The sacrificial system comes to an abrupt end. The priests' gig is up.

Jesus will assign His apostles as the new tenants, the new religious leaders who will guide and care for God's people. The Church, led by Peter and the apostles, will bring good fruits of repentance and righteousness in the lives of believers. Instead of the sacrificial system, offering to God unblemished lambs, Jesus will make the perfect sacrifice of atonement to God the Father for the sins of the world. Jesus is the Lamb of God who takes away the sins of the world. Jesus leaves the Eucharist, His body, blood, soul, and divinity to nourish and sustain those who follow Him.

1. How will the Messiah come?

Isaiah 62:11–12
Zechariah 9:9
Matthew 21:1–5

2. How will Jerusalem welcome her Messiah?

Psalm 118:26–27
Matthew 21:6–11
CCC 559–560

3. Find and explain a significant title for Jesus.

Matthew 21:9, 15
CCC 439

4. How would you answer the question *"Who is this?"* (Matthew 21:10)

5. Explain the drama in Matthew 21:12–13.

6. What is the significance of the Temple? Matthew 21:12–13

Isaiah 56:7
Jeremiah 7:11
CCC 584
CCC 586

* Where does God dwell now? How do you care for His temple? 2 Corinthians 6:16

7. How do the chief priests respond to Jesus? Matthew 21:14–16

8. How does Jesus respond to the religious leaders?

Psalm 8:1–2
Matthew 21:16–17

** How do you react to babies and infants in church? Pray about your answer.

9. Who and how does Jesus invite people to enter His kingdom? CCC 544, 546

10. Explain the drama in Matthew 21:18–20.

11. What can you learn about prayer?

Matthew 21:21–22
James 1:5–6, 5:16
CCC 2610–2611

* When people ask you to pray for them, how do you remember to intercede?

12. Explain the drama in Matthew 21:23–27.

13. How does Jesus trap the religious leaders? Matthew 21:24–27

14. Explain the parable of the two sons. Matthew 21:28–30

15. Why are sinners entering the kingdom of heaven? Matthew 21:31–32

16. Who does the son in the parable, represent?

Matthew 21:33–39
Matthew 3:17

17. What will happen to the tenants (religious leaders)? Matthew 21:40–41

18. What does the vineyard, cultivated field, and building represent and foretell?

CCC 755
CCC 756

19. What can you learn from these verses?

Psalm 118:22–23
Matthew 21:42
Acts 4:10–12
1 Peter 2:6–8

20. What is the cornerstone of your life? Describe your time, talent, and treasure.

CHAPTER 17

Questions
Matthew 22

*"Render therefore to Caesar the things that are Caesar's,
and to God the things that are God's."*
Matthew 22:21

The Greek philosopher Socrates developed a method of teaching based on a series of questions and answers. The wise questioner helps an individual or group arrive at a satisfactory set of conclusions by eliminating one hypothesis after another. At times Jesus uses this question-and-answer method with His disciples: "Who do people say that I am? Who do you say that I am?" Sometimes, the Pharisees try to use this method on Jesus. This interactive kind of teaching engages the minds of the students more fully than a lecture or homily, and helps them formulate solutions for themselves rather than being handed answers on a silver platter.

Greek rhetoricians posed questions with obvious answers. The technical term for this figure of speech is *Erotesis,* or Interrogation. The name Michael exemplifies this kind of question—*Who is like God?* (Daniel 10:13, 21, 12:1). Other such questions are: *Who is like you?* (Exodus 15:11; Psalm 35:10, 71:19), *Who is like the Lord our God?* (Psalm 113:5), and *Who in the skies can be compared to the Lord?* (Psalm 89:6). The answer to all these questions is the same: obviously—no one. Such a reply, however, ends the train of thought. The Socratic method, on the contrary, usually involved a series of questions, with each answer suggesting the next question, until only one solution was possible at the end.

"Friend, how did you get in here without a wedding garment?" (Matthew 22:12).
What kind of question is this? — A polite question.
Who asks the question? — The father-in-law of the groom.
Who answers it? — The man who crashed the wedding party.
What is the right answer? — "I'd be happy to put on a garment right away!"

Jesus himself poses this question, in the parable about a king who gave a wedding party for his son. No invited guests came, so he sent messengers to the highways to bring in the general public. One man, however, came in without a proper garment. In those days hosts provided garments for their guests. Some guests came from a distance, riding in carts or on animals, or walking on dusty roads. Their traveling clothes were dusty, dirty, and maybe even unsanitary. They would bathe their feet and hands, and slip on a nice, clean garment provided by the hosts. One expense of putting on a wedding feast was renting wedding garments for the guests.

The man in the parable had insulted the bride and groom, their families, and all the wedding guests, by refusing to put on the proper garment that was provided at the door. The king wants to know if the man had some good reason, and so he poses the question, *"How did you get in here without a wedding garment?"* (Matthew 22:12). When the man has no reasonable justification to give, he is thrown out.

What garments does our soul need to wear to be suitable for the kingdom of God? The Old Testament says that we are to be clothed with garments of salvation and wrapped with a robe of righteousness (Isaiah 61:10), adorned with eminence and dignity, clothed with honor and majesty (Job 40:10), and girded with gladness (Psalm 30:11). The New Testament says that we are to be clothed with power from on high (Luke 24:49), clothed with the armor of light (Romans 13:12), clothed with Christ (Romans 13:14, Galatians 3:27), girded with truth (Ephesians 6:14), and clothed with humility (1 Peter 5:5). Are you properly attired for heaven?

Those are the garments of grace! Jesus poured forth blood and water from his side on the Cross to provide the sacramental graces with which He wants to clothe us—Baptism, Confirmation, Eucharist, Confession, Anointing of the Sick, Matrimony, Holy Orders. How foolish to try and carry on bravely by our own strength when the strength of God is available. We should let Christ keep our souls in a state of grace, so that we will be ever ready to celebrate the wedding feast of the Lamb.

"Is it lawful to pay taxes to Caesar, or not?" (Matthew 22:17).
      What kind of question is this? — A trick question.
      Who asks the question? — Disciples of the Pharisees, and the Herodians.
      Who answers it? — Jesus
      What is the right answer? — He answers with another question.

The Pharisees and Herodians pose a question intended to make Jesus look bad no matter how he answers it. If He answers in the affirmative, that it is lawful to pay taxes to Caesar, then He would be siding with the tax collectors, who raised money to pay for the occupying Roman army; He would lose his bona fide claim to the throne of David by supporting an alien king. If, on the other hand, He answers in the negative, then He would look like a tax protestor, a zealot, and a troublemaker, and then He could be arrested for encouraging insurrection.

Several times in the gospels, people ask Jesus this kind of a no-win question, where He would be damned if He said "yes," and damned if He said "no." Never once, however, do they succeed in cornering Jesus; never once does He fall into their traps. He shows Himself so dexterous in pirouetting out of these situations, walking away unscathed. He promised that He would send His Spirit so that His followers too could find words, and wisdom that no one could contradict.

"Why put me to the test, you hypocrites?" (Matthew 22:18).
      What kind of question is this? — A personal question.
      Who asks the question? — Jesus.
      Who answers it? — No one.
      What is the right answer? — Because they want to trap Jesus in His speech.

With this rhetorical question, Jesus exposes the insincerity of the questioners. He does not let them hide their ill will behind a seemingly innocent question. They have asked not out of desire for truth or even idle curiosity. The word for "test" in Hebrew is the same as the word for "temptation." These questioners are functioning like a Satan, or "interrogator" in Hebrew. He calls them hypocrites because someone else has set them up to ask the question; they are not even asking on their own behalf. They are pawns of the evil one.

Without a pause, Jesus keeps the dialogue moving by asking them to show Him the money for the tax. Without thinking, they reach into their pockets and take out a Roman coin, with images of gods, goddesses and emperors on it. For them even to touch such a coin involved them in the sin of idolatry. That is why tax collectors were excommunicated, because they had to handle such coins all the time. Jesus unmasks them as more interested in money than in truth. Although they tried to throw Him off the cliff, He has regained the high ground.

"Whose likeness and inscription is this?" (Matthew 22:20).
> What kind of question is this? — A revealing question.
> Who asks the question? — Jesus.
> Who answers it? — Disciples of the Pharisees, along with the Herodians.
> What is the right answer? — The likeness is Caesar's.

Thus Jesus concludes this series of three questions, to render unto Caesar what is Caesar's, but unto God what is God's. Now there were two kinds of tax at the time —imperial tax, and temple tax. The first went to support the civil administration and the military, the second to support the temple and its charitable causes. Imperial coinage, with images of gods and emperors, could not pay the temple tax; they had to be changed into specially minted coins. So on one level, Jesus is pointing out that the coin in question was appropriate to pay one kind of tax but not another.

On another level, however, Jesus is making a general statement about our obligations to the state. The state has real rights to receive fiscal support of the citizenry for the sake of the common good. Paul passes on the instruction of Christ in this form: *You also pay taxes, for the authorities are ministers of God, attending to this very thing. Pay all of them their dues, taxes to whom taxes are due, revenue to whom revenue is due, respect to whom respect is due, honor to whom honor is due* (Romans 13:6–7). Taxes go to the state, but what belongs to God?

God has a prior claim by being the source of all blessings, while states provide only limited benefits. Paul proudly exercised his rights of Roman citizenship, but he also wrote: *Our commonwealth is in heaven, and from it we await a Savior, the Lord Jesus Christ* (Philippians 3:20). Every Christian has dual citizenship, born or naturalized as citizens of earthly nations, but also by virtue of Baptism being citizens of the Kingdom. Separation of church and state is not a division of equals; human governments will pass away, but divine governance will not. We give Caesar what is Caesar's as long as we have Caesar, but we will give God what is God's forever.

A few years after Paul wrote those letters to the Philippians and to the Romans, the relationship between religion and the empire took a serious turn for the worse. The Judeans rebelled, the temple was destroyed, and Judaism lost the support of state taxation. Living emperors began to demand that incense be offered to them as gods, something that Christians could never give. God never takes from Caesar, but Caesar often tries to take away what belongs to God.

Worship of the state became a common theme again during the twentieth century. The good Russian people who used say *Slava* (Glory) to God alone, were forced to say it to Lenin and Stalin instead. Fifteen thousand Spanish priests and nuns died rather than renounce the Lord. Whenever Caesar has demanded all the glory, the Christians have always insisted on rendering to God what belongs to God alone.

"In the resurrection . . . to which of the seven will she be wife?" (Matthew 22:28).
    What kind of question is this? — A tough question.
    Who asks the question? — Sadducees.
    Who answers it? — Jesus.
    What is the right answer? — In the resurrection they do not marry.

When the Sadducees heard that Jesus had bested the Pharisees, they thought to enlist Him to their cause. So they gave Him the toughest question they could muster. The Sadducees did not believe in the resurrection of the dead on the last day, so they gave Jesus a question that seemed to have stumped the Pharisees to date. If a man married seven wives over the course of his life, maybe he could have seven wives in heaven. Jesus goes to the root of the case, and says that neither men nor women will marry in heaven, because marriage is contracted until death do us part. Some never remarry after the death of a spouse, because of loyalty to their memory. Though free to remarry, they choose not to do so. Many widows lived in the Holy Land, to be near the temple, like Anna the prophetess (Luke 2:36); many widows followed Jesus and continued to build up the church. Jesus' answer to the Sadducees supported those widows in their choice to remain alone, so that holy widowhood became in the early church a kind of religious vocation.

"Teacher, which is the greatest commandment in the law?" (Matthew 22:36).
    What kind of question is this? — A key question.
    Who asks the question? — A lawyer.
    Who answers it? — Jesus.
    What is the right answer? — Love your Lord, and love your neighbor.

After Jesus supported a bodily resurrection against the Sadducees, a legal scholar allied to the Pharisees approached to test him. Jesus chose to overlook his motives and to consider the question on its own merits. Luke's parallel account concludes with the Parable of the Good Samaritan (Luke 10:25-37).

The Pharisees tried to apply the Torah to daily life, and the people wanted to know where they should start—with moral laws, kosher laws, marriage laws, ritual laws, economic laws, and so on. So scholars discussed among themselves how to prioritize the hundreds of laws that were on the books. Although Jesus sparred with the Pharisees on a number of occasions, His teachings had more in common with theirs than with any other sect in Judaism of the time. On this occasion, the answer that Jesus gives is exactly the same as the one that became normative for Rabbinic Judaism, namely, that the greatest emphasis should go to the love of God (Deuteronomy 6:5) and to the love of neighbor (Leviticus 19:18).

"What do you think of the Christ? Whose son is he?" (Matthew 22:42).
    What kind of question is this? — A double question.
    Who asks the question? — Jesus
    Who answers it? — Pharisees.
    What is the right answer? — Christ is the son of David.

This chapter of questions draws toward a close now with a Messianic analysis. Nathan the Prophet had told David that a son of his would sit upon his throne (1 Kings 9:5; Psalm 132:12), and so everyone knew that the Messiah would belong to the line of David. Every king who ruled at Jerusalem for five hundred years belonged to the House of David, making it one of the longest dynasties in the ancient world. At the very beginning of this Gospel, the genealogy of Jesus establishes that He inherits the throne of Israel, through Joseph, going back fourteen generations to the Babylonian exile and fourteen further generations before that to Solomon and David. That list circulated among Messianic Jews at the time, who needed to know who was in line for the throne of David. Therefore, the answer to this question is clearly the easiest in this whole chapter: the Christ is to be the son of David. The easy question is merely a prelude, however, stipulating the facts that will form the basis of another question that is much more difficult.

"If David thus calls him Lord, how is he his son?" (Matthew 22:45).
    What kind of question is this? — A paradoxical question.
    Who asks the question? — Jesus.
    Who answers it? — No one.
    What is the right answer? — Christ has greater authority than King David.

By the end of the chapter, Jesus has stumped everyone. No one can answer His query about why David calls his offspring "Lord:" *The* LORD *says to my Lord* (Psalm 110:1). Princes call their royal father "Lord," but kings do not address their royal sons that way. Only by the development of Christian doctrine has an explanation come about for the passage. The divine nature of Christ invites the human nature of Christ to sit upon the throne of heaven, so that now and forever, the two natures of Christ exercise sovereignty over all. A magnificent medieval drawing portrays the two natures—true God and true man—as mirror images of each other, seated side-by-side, with the enemies beneath their feet.

Questions used to be associated with the Sacrament of Confirmation, when the bishop would interrogate the candidates with questions from the Baltimore Catechism.

Questions still have a formal role to play in the Liturgy of Easter and in the Sacrament of Baptism, when the candidates and their sponsors answer, "I do," to each of these six Baptismal Promises:

— Do you reject Satan?

— And all his works?

— And all his empty promises?

— Do you believe in God the Father, creator of heaven and earth?

— Do you believe in Jesus Christ, his Son, our Lord, who was conceived by the Holy Spirit, born of the Virgin Mary, suffered under Pontius Pilate, was crucified, died and was buried, rose from the dead and is seated now at the right hand of the Father?

— Do you believe in the Holy Spirit, the Holy Catholic Church, the Communion of Saints, the forgiveness of sins and life everlasting?

Everyone has been put on this earth for the purpose of answering one and the same question: Which side are you on? On the side of good or the side of evil? Every created being capable of moral judgment has to answer this question, from the very angels of God on down to us mere mortals. Unfortunately, at the dawn of creation, the human race made a bad judgment call, and started a downward slide in which self-worship translated increasingly into hatred of one another and of God. God so loved the world, however, that He sent His only-begotten Son that the world might be saved and redirected towards love of God and neighbor. The Holy Spirit pours into our hearts a new spirit, the supernatural gift of Divine Love.

So now the question has taken on a more precise form: Which side are you on? Are you on the side of love or on the side of hatred? We answer this question not by crying "Lord, Lord," but by the cumulative effect of a lifetime of choices, large and small. Small acts of selfishness lead to heartless mortal sins and an ultimate compact with evil. Small acts of kindness lead to genuine sacrifices that establish an eternal bond of goodness. If, in the last moment of our life, the fundamental question presents itself to us, an Act of Love might make an excellent answer:

O Lord God, I love you above all things
and I love my neighbor for your sake
Because you are the highest, infinite and perfect good,
worthy of all my love.
In this love I intend to live and die. Amen.

1. Why does Jesus use parables? Matthew 22:1–14, CCC 546

2. What is the significance of marital (bride and bridegroom) imagery?

Matthew 22:1–11
Revelation 22:17
CCC 796

3. What do the Pharisees try to do to Jesus with their questions? Matthew 22:15, 18

4. What do they say about Jesus? Matthew 22:16

5. How should Christians respond to civil authorities and to God?

Matthew 22:21
Romans 13:7
CCC 2242

* Can you think of a time in which it would be moral to disobey the civil law?

6. What belongs to God?

Psalm 139:1–16
1 Corinthians 3:16
1 Corinthians 6:19–20

* In what ways can you glorify God in your body, practically?

7. What issue emerges in these passages?

Matthew 22:23–33
CCC 575
Acts 4:1–2
Acts 4:8–10

8. How did the Jewish leaders address Jesus?

Matthew 22:16b, 23b
Matthew 22:35
CCC 581

9. What question is asked in Matthew 22:36?

10. How does Jesus respond?

Matthew 22:37
Deuteronomy 6:5
CCC 2055
CCC 2083

* How can you practically love God with your whole heart, soul, and mind?

11. What else does Jesus add?

Matthew 22:38–40
Leviticus 19:18

12. What does loving your neighbor accomplish? CCC 1823–1825

* Practically, how can you love your neighbor?

13. What does Saint Paul add to this? Galatians 5:14–15

14. What does Saint James add to this command? James 2:8–9

15. What fulfills the law? Romans 13:8–10

16. How does Jesus turn the tables on the Pharisees? Matthew 22:41–45

17. What can you learn about Jesus from Hebrews 1:8–13?

18. How does Saint Peter explain these verses? Acts 2:29–36

19. For what were the Jews waiting and hoping? CCC 439

20. What is the significance of the title "Lord?"

Matthew 22:44–45
CCC 447–448
CCC 449–450

CHAPTER 18

Lament over Jerusalem
Matthew 23

"O Jerusalem, Jerusalem, killing the prophets
and stoning those who are sent to you!
How often would I have gathered your children together
as a hen gathers her brood under her wings, and you would not!
Behold, your house is forsaken and desolate.
For I tell you, you will not see me again, until you say,
'Blessed is he who comes in the name of the Lord.'"
Matthew 23:37–39

Jesus denounces the hypocrisy of the scribes and Pharisees—By reporting Jesus' harsh language in this chapter, Matthew has been accused of being anti-Semitic. However, Jesus, Peter, Matthew himself, a Jewish tax collector, and all of the apostles are Jews. Sadly, people have distorted these verses to rationalize persecution of the Jews over the centuries, which the Catholic Church decries. Saint John Paul II publicly asked forgiveness for all acts of anti-Semitism perpetrated by Christians in history. Jesus' harsh condemnation of the scribes and Pharisees is not directed at their ethnic identity, but at their unrepentant sinful conduct.

> The Church does not hesitate to impute to Christians the gravest responsibility for the torments inflicted upon Jesus, a responsibility with which they have all too often burdened the Jews alone. . . . Since our sins made the Lord Christ suffer the torment of the cross, those who plunge themselves into disorders and crimes crucify the Son of God anew in their hearts (for he is in them) and hold him up to contempt. And it can be seen that our crime in this case is greater in us than in the Jews. CCC 598

Prophets of the Old Testament voiced similar strong, harsh language to confront sinful Israel. Often woes, strong rebukes, and correction preceded adversity, or a punishment from God upon the rebellious people.

+ *Woe to the wicked!* (Isaiah 3:11).
+ *Woe to those who call evil good and good evil* (Isaiah 5:20).
+ *Woe to those who are wise in their own eyes* (Isaiah 5:21).
+ *Woe to you, O Jerusalem! How long will it be before you are made clean?* (Jeremiah 13:27).
+ *Woe to them, for they have strayed from me!* (Hosea 7:13).
+ *Woe to those who devise wickedness and work evil* (Micah 2:1).

Formerly, Jesus and the elders have had civil discourse. But now, Jesus uses strong prophetic language to denounce the religious leaders who sit on Moses' seat. Moses' seat may be an actual chair, used in the synagogue for the one authorized to teach Mosaic Law, or it may be a metaphor for authority. Jesus tells the crowds and disciples to obey sound religious instruction, but not to imitate hypocritical practices. The religious leaders are guilty of leading double lives. They proclaim pious ideals in public, but behave sinfully themselves.

These religious leaders impose heavy burdens on people, but will not help them at all. Whereas, Jesus' burden is light (Matthew 11:30) and He sends the Holy Spirit to help believers (Matthew 3:11; 28:19). Phylacteries are small leather boxes containing Scriptures, strapped between the forehead and arm during prayer (Exodus 13:9, Deuteronomy 6:8). The Pharisees made them larger and more noticeable, along with lengthening the tassels on their prayer shawls. *Rabbi* came to be a term used for teacher, but literally in Hebrew it means "my great one."

Once again, Jesus uses hyperbole, *"Call no man your father on earth, for you have one Father, who is in heaven"* (Matthew 23:9). The early Christian community understood Jesus' intent in this passage, and did not hesitate to call spiritual leaders "father." Paul says: *For I became your father in Christ Jesus through the gospel* (1 Corinthians 4:15b), and *I appeal to you for my child, Onesimus, whose father I have become* (Philemon 10). While Catholics know that God is our Father in heaven, we call our male parent "father," and we respectfully call ordained priests on earth "Father."

The Pharisees fail to observe Jesus' model of servant leadership. Leaders must be servants of others. Those who exalt themselves will be humbled, but God exalts the humble. *Pride goes before destruction, and a haughty spirit before a fall* (Proverbs 16:18). *A man's pride will bring him low, but he who is lowly in spirit will obtain honor* (Proverbs 29:23). The Pharisees demonstrate pride and arrogance.

Seven woes contrast with the blessings Jesus pronounced in the Sermon on the Mount. Jesus uses extremely harsh language to condemn the Pharisees' practices.
1) *"Woe to you, scribes and Pharisees, hypocrites! because you shut the kingdom of heaven against men"* (Matthew 23:13). Because of their scrupulous demands, the Pharisees made it virtually impossible for people to come into a relationship with God. Christians rely on God's grace.
2) *"Woe to you, scribes and Pharisees, hypocrites! . . . you traverse sea and land to make a single proselyte . . . you make him [the convert] twice as much a child of hell as yourselves"* (Matthew 23:15). Hell is real. Do not end up there, and do not lead others into perdition either.
3) *"Woe to you, blind guides"* who make a mockery of promises and construct legalistic distinctions for oaths (Matthew 23:16–22). Just honor your word. James exhorts, *let your yes be yes and your no be no* (James 5:12).
4) *"Woe to you, scribes and Pharisees, hypocrites! for you tithe mint and cummin, and have neglected . . . justice and mercy and faith"* (Matthew 23:23). Mint and cumin are tiny spices compared to a camel, a huge, unclean animal. The Pharisees would strain their wine to screen out a tiny insect, but ignore the larger, more important matters of faith, justice, and mercy.

5) *"Woe to you, scribes and Pharisees, hypocrites! for you cleanse the outside of the cup and of the plate, but inside they are full of extortion and rapacity"* (Matthew 23:25). Looking good on the outside cannot fool God, who sees the heart. Leaders and believers must be transparent—pure inside and out.

6) *"Woe to you, scribes and Pharisees, hypocrites! for you are like whitewashed tombs, which outwardly appear beautiful, but within they are full of dead men's bones and all uncleanness"* (Matthew 23:27). Painting tombstones to make them look nice does not alter the bodies decaying inside. The Pharisees would whitewash tombstones to prevent people from inadvertently touching them and becoming ritually unclean. But, a decaying soul is far worse.

7) *"Woe to you, scribes and Pharisees, hypocrites! . . . I send you prophets and wise men and scribes, some of whom you will kill and crucify, and some you will scourge in your synagogues and persecute"* (Matthew 23:29, 34). The Catholic Church will be a suffering, persecuted Church.

"That upon you may come all the righteous blood shed on earth, from the blood of innocent Abel to the blood of Zechariah the son of Barachiah, whom you murdered between the sanctuary and the altar" (Matthew 23:35). The first part of this verse refers clearly to Cain's fratricide of his brother Abel (Genesis 4:8–10), the first murder reported in the Bible. However, the second part proves difficult to understand. Since the Bible does not record this martyrdom, Matthew relies on rabbinic tradition, which reports that Zechariah was murdered in the Temple.

The final woe recalls the persecution of prophets of old, and alerts the disciples to the type of death that Jesus will endure—scourging and crucifixion, and the persecution that they also will endure after Jesus' death. All of the apostles, except John, will be martyred. Every Pope for the first two centuries of Christianity will be martyred, as well. Jesus does not promise a rose garden or a prosperity gospel.

The Lament over Jerusalem—*"O Jerusalem, Jerusalem, killing the prophets and stoning those who are sent to you! How often would I have gathered your children together as a hen gathers her brood under her wings, and you would not! Behold, your house is forsaken and desolate. For I tell you, you will not see me again, until you say, 'Blessed is he who comes in the name of the Lord'"* (Matthew 23:37–39).

King Solomon (970–931 BC) built the magnificent temple in Jerusalem, to honor God. This spectacular temple was dedicated in 953 BC, after years of quarrying stone, importing cedars from Lebanon, and using the finest materials and most skilled craftsmen. God dwelt in His temple, a place for prayer, worship, teaching, and sacrificing animals to God. Nebuchadnezzar destroyed the temple in 586 BC and exiled the inhabitants of Jerusalem to Babylon. The splendid temple lay in ruins for years until King Cyrus of Persia came to power. Ezra and Nehemiah obtained permission to re-build the temple.

The temple was rebuilt and re-dedicated in 520 BC, with the sacred vessels returned, and an opportunity for worship and sacrifice to continue. However, the second temple was not as spectacular as Solomon's temple. At least, the pilgrims could go to the place where God dwelt, worship, and offer sacrifice. The second temple was being renovated in Jesus' time. But, as Jesus foretold, the temple and Jerusalem would be destroyed in AD 70, only two decades after the Crucifixion. Only part of the western wall of the temple remains today.

Jesus used Old Testament images and the literary form of apostrophe to speak about Jerusalem, a city, as if speaking to her inhabitants. *Like birds hovering, so the L*ORD *of hosts will protect Jerusalem* (Isaiah 31:5). *How precious is your mercy, O God! The children of men take refuge in the shadow of your wings* (Psalm 36:7). Although God desires to show mercy to the scribes and Pharisees, to the inhabitants of Jerusalem, and to all people, free will cannot be revoked. People still have the power to reject God's mercy and forgiveness.

The Name of God is Mercy

Sometimes when Christians think like scholars of the law, their hearts extinguish that which the Holy Spirit lights up in the heart of a sinner when he stands at the threshold when he starts to feel nostalgia for God. . . . Hypocrites are men who live attached to the letter of the law but who neglect love . . .

Matthew describes those who tie up heavy burdens and lay them on other men's shoulders . . . and want to be called master. This conduct comes when a person loses the sense of awe for salvation that has been granted to him. When a person feels more secure, he begins to appropriate faculties which are not his own, but which are the Lord's. The awe seems to fade, and this is the basis for clericalism or for the conduct of people who feel pure. What then prevails is a formal adherence to rules. . . . And if that person is a minister of God, he ends up believing that he is separate from the people, that he owns the doctrine, that he owns power, and he closes himself off from God's surprises.

The repentant sinner, who sins again and again because of his weakness, will find forgiveness if he acknowledges his need for mercy. The corrupt man is the one who sins but does not repent, who sins and pretends to be Christian, and it is this double life that is scandalous. The corrupt man does not know humility, he does not consider himself in need of help; he leads a double life. The corrupt man often doesn't realize his own condition, much as a person with bad breath does not know they have it. And it is not easy for the corrupt man to get out of this state by feeling inner remorse. Generally, the Lord saves him through life's great ordeals, situations that he cannot avoid and which crack open the shell that he has gradually built up, thus allowing the Grace of God to enter.

Pope Francis, *The Name of God is Mercy,*
(New York: Random Books, 2016), 68, 81, 84

1. What advice does Jesus give in Matthew 23:1–3?

2. Compare the following passages.

Matthew 23:4
Acts 15:10–11

3. How do contemporary people make a show of their religion? Matthew 23:5–7

4. What can you learn about "fathers" from these passages?

Matthew 23:9
Acts 7:2; 22:1
Ephesians 6:4
Hebrews 12:9

5. Who is invited to share in the fatherhood of God? CCC 2367

* What do you call the man who provided you with natural life and the man who brings you spiritual life?

6. How do you become a child of God? CCC 526, 1213

7. How can you become "great" in the kingdom of God? Matthew 23:10–12

* What practical things can you do to humble yourself? 1 Peter 5:6

8. What do Jesus' woes warn against?

Matthew 23:13–19
CCC 2111

** What are some current superstitions to avoid?

9. Is Jesus hostile to the temple?

Matthew 23:20–21
CCC 586

10. Should Christians swear and make oaths? James 5:12

11. Explain Jesus' next woe. To whom is it directed? Matthew 23:23–24

12. What three things does God require of you? Micah 6:8

13. Use a dictionary or the Catechism to define "justice." CCC 1807

14. Use a dictionary or the Catechism to define "mercy." CCC 1829

* List practical ways to show justice.

15. List ways of offering mercy below. Choose one and do it. CCC 2447

Corporal Works of Mercy	Spiritual Works of Mercy

16. How can one avoid the woe described in Matthew 23:25–26?

Matthew 23:25–26
Proverbs 4:23

17. Compare the following verses.

Psalm 5:9
Matthew 23:27–28

18. Explain the following verses.

Matthew 23:29–35
Acts 7:51–53

19. How does Jesus feel about Jerusalem? Matthew 23:37

20. What is the hope of Israel?

Matthew 23:38–39
Psalm 118:25–26
CCC 674

CHAPTER 19

The End Time
Matthew 24–25

"Heaven and earth will pass away,
but my words will not pass away."
Matthew 24:35

On one occasion, Jesus wept when He foresaw the destruction of Jerusalem (Luke 19:41). So, He certainly took no pleasure in announcing to the apostles that the holy temple, the dwelling place of God on earth, the object of their loyalty and affection, would be overturned, stone by stone. After all, Jesus called the temple: *"My Father's house"* (Luke 2:49, John 2:16). He revealed these premonitions of destruction in about AD 30–33. The temple was demolished in AD 70. The timespan between the prophecy and its fulfillment, then, was about forty years.

"What will be the sign of your coming and of the close of the age?" (Matthew 24:3). The apostles ask Jesus about the end times, and He answers them with a long discourse about pain and agony, signs and portents. He never called Himself a prophet; He usually gave instructions about inner life and heavenly life, rather than future earthly life. Here, He makes an exception. The apostles have asked an important question, and He honors them with a serious reply.

"For many will come in my name, saying 'I am the Christ'" (Matthew 24:5). A few verses later Jesus uses the term *false Christs* (Matthew 24:24), or *pseudochristoi* in the Greek. The term means someone who lays claim to the Throne of David without having that right. The first pseudo-Christs were the pathetic dynasts of Northern Israel after they split off from the House of David. In the second century BC the Hasmoneans, of the Tribe of Levi, took the throne illicitly. At the time Jesus was speaking, the Herodians, who were only half Judean, were ruling. The prophecy of Jesus proves true in the subsequent history of the Jewish people, who have been disappointed repeatedly by messianic imposters and false claimants. Many Jews have lapsed from the practice of their faith as a result of these abused hopes.

Jesus never uses the term antichrist in the Gospels. In his letters, John, the only New Testament author to do so, speaks of *many antichrists* (1 John 2:18), defined as *he who denies that Jesus is the Christ* (1 John 2:22), and also of the *spirit of the antichrist* (1 John 4:3). In his second letter, John speaks of *many deceivers*, but of one who is to be *the deceiver and the antichrist* (2 John 7). Many Christians have applied this terminology to the great *beast with seven heads and ten horns* in Revelation 17:7, who is expected to be the last and worst of the pseudo-Christs.

"Then they will deliver you up to tribulation, and put you to death" (Matthew 24:9). According to tradition, ten of the twelve apostles were put to death for their faith in Christ.

The two exceptions are Judas Iscariot the betrayer, and John, who survived the attempts to kill him. Peter serves as the Vicar of Christ for forty years, the longest papacy in history, but he too suffers martyrdom at the onset of the Era of Persecutions. That era still continues, wherever bishops are jailed (China), conversion is forbidden (India), celebration of Mass is banned (Saudi Arabia), and populations are cleansed (Middle East). There is little wonder that Christ has delayed His return, considering how badly everyone treated Him the first time, and how ready many would be to do it again if given a chance.

"And many false prophets will arise" (Matthew 24:11). God has not chosen to reveal beforehand the identity of the false prophet and the antichrist. The false prophet is easy to recognize. True prophets cannot be wrong, so long as they say only what they hear from God. False prophets are not credible, even if they accidentally get something right once in a while, because they invent all of it. The greatest of the true prophets was John the Baptist, who pointed out Jesus as the Messiah, when He came. The greatest of the false prophets, at the end time, will point to an impostor as the messiah. Doing the bidding of the Father of Lies, he will also accuse many people of being the antichrist, and detract attention away from the evil one. He will portray good people as bad, and paint bad people as good.

"The sun will be darkened" (Matthew 24:29). Every day, the sun darkens from sundown to sunrise, as well as during cloud cover. More terrifying are solar eclipses, when the moon blocks sunlight from reaching the earth. The Greek historian Herodotus records that battling Medes and Lydians put down their arms and made peace when the sun eclipsed on 28 May 585 BC, and that solar eclipses accompanied the Persian invasions of Greece on 2 October 480 BC and 1 August 477 BC. During a total solar eclipse in the United States on 26 February 1979, a young Father Ponessa happened to look out the window of his classroom at Central Catholic High School, and said, "You've got to see this!" Students rose from their desks to view downtown Billings, Montana, bathed in spooky, gray light.

"And the moon will not give its light" (Matthew 24:29). The moon fades to total darkness at the end of every lunar month, so dark moons occur at regular intervals, every 29.53 days. At such times, the moon continues to shine, but is no longer visible from the earth. More drastic are the lunar eclipses, which take place when the earth blocks sunlight from reaching the moon. During the life of Jesus, inhabitants of the Holy Land witnessed one total lunar eclipse on 13 March 4 BC, and one partial eclipse on 10 January 1 BC. One month after the Emperor Augustus died, Roman legionaries stationed in what is now Hungary witnessed a lunar eclipse on 14 September AD 14, took it as a bad omen, and mutinied against their commanders. Celestial changes can be terrifying in every age.

"And the stars will fall from heaven" (Matthew 24:29). The sudden falling of meteors from the sky was held to be a very bad omen, but comets were more ambiguous. Halley's Comet appeared at both the beginning and at the end of New Testament times, the first appearance recorded by Chinese astronomers on 10 October 12 BC, and the second reported by Rabbi Yehoshua ben Hananiah in the Talmud, on 25 January AD 66. The same comet last came on 9 February 1986 and will reappear on 28 July 2061. The Magi from the East were experts in predicting and interpreting such celestial signs.

"And the powers of heaven will be shaken" (Matthew 24:29). The term *powers of heaven* may refer to the planets, which Gentiles worshipped as gods. However, they always have wandering trajectories anyway. More likely Jesus here refers to constellations, which hold fixed positions in the sky, though Northern and Southern Hemispheres have different stars overhead. In this interpretation, shaking the powers of heaven would mean shifting the axial tilt of the earth itself. Normally there are small variances in the ecliptic, but the moon provides a stabilizing effect. Were the moon to disappear, the earth's obliquity would become less regular. The effects, needless to say, would be catastrophic for all life on earth.

"He will send out his angels with a loud trumpet call" (Matthew 24:31). A ram's horn was blown at New Year, and ancient generals used trumpets to send military commands to their troops, so the trumpet will sound at the beginning of the final battle for the planet. Like Jesus, Paul describes the end in musical terms: *In a moment, in the twinkling of an eye, at the last trumpet. For the trumpet will sound, and the dead will be raised imperishable, and we shall be changed* (1 Corinthians 15:52). The loud trumpet call of the angels will signal the *parousia,* the Second Coming of Christ in glory, the final judgment, and the end time.

> In the last days, then, false prophets and corrupters will be multiplied. Sheep will be turned into wolves and charity will be turned into hate. As lawlessness increases, men will hate one another and persecute and betray; and then will appear the deceiver of the world as a Son of God. He will work signs and wonders and the world will be given over into his hands. He will do such wicked deeds as have not been done since the world began. Then will all created men come to the fire of judgment, and many will be scandalized and will be lost; but those who persevere in their faith, will be saved out from under the accursed thing itself.
>
> *Didache or Teaching of the Twelve Apostles* (AD 140), 16.3

First Narrative—*"From the fig tree learn its lesson"* (Matthew 24:32). Jesus now continues His teaching on the end time with a set of five allegorical narratives, only two in strict parable form. Luke gives two fig parables (Luke 13:6–9; 21:29–33), the second of which reads: *Look at the fig tree, and all the trees* (Luke 21:29). The three fruits commonly grown in the Mediterranean are the fig, vine, and olive. Like bananas, figs continue ripening after they are picked, and so can be harvested before other fruits. That makes them a most useful fruit to illustrate getting ready.

Second Narrative—*"Who then is the faithful and wise servant?"* (Matthew 24:45). Masters and servants figure in several of the parables. At the end time, Jesus wants to discover people prepared like the diligent and faithful servant. They will be praised and rewarded, while the lax servants will be punished. This narrative has moved from agricultural to sociological imagery, but retains exactly the same moral message as the preceding. Keep the faith. Be faithful and persevere.

Third Narrative—"*Then the kingdom of heaven shall be compared to ten maidens*" (Matthew 25:1). The use of the formula "shall be compared to" puts this narrative into strict parable form. The comparison is between the kingdom of heaven and a wedding reception. Recall three chapters ago the parable of the wedding guest who entered the reception without a proper garment (Matthew 22:11). That guest was like the five foolish maidens; the other guests were like the five wise maidens. Again this parable is about preparation. Jesus warns believers to be ready and waiting.

Wedding banquets were then and still are the biggest social events in most peoples' lives, bringing together two families and many friends. Jesus and Mary honored the couple in Cana by sharing their celebration. When Jesus sets His parables in wedding receptions, He identifies the kingdom as the place of major celebration. Heaven itself comes to be called *the marriage supper of the Lamb* (Revelation 19:9).

Fourth Narrative—"*For it will be as when a man going on a journey called his servants and entrusted to them his property*" (Matthew 25:14). Jesus employs the word "as" here, and "it" refers back to the previous parable. So this too is a kingdom parable, which speaks of the reward or punishment for those who have used or not used their talents. The great sin in this parable is the sin of omission. The king asks not what commands have been disobeyed, but what use has been made of opportunities given. People will also be judged on what they fail to do.

Fifth Narrative—"*He will separate them one from another as a shepherd separates the sheep from the goats*" (Matthew 25:32). Jesus now tells of the Last Judgment in a pure narrative form, except for two verses with vivid images of sheep and goats. In the Torah both sheep and goats are clean animals, kosher for the Hebrew table. Even the Passover lamb may come from either the sheep or the goats (Exodus 12:1–20). So these goats in this parable are not predestined to condemnation by their nature, which came clean from the Creator. It is not *who they are* that brings judgment, but what they have failed to do for their neighbor. Again the wicked are lost not for the evil they have done, but for the good that they have neglected to do.

> Come, He says, inherit the kingdom. What honor, what blessedness have these words! For He says not, Take, but Inherit as one's own, as your Father's, as yours, as due you from the first. For He says, before you existed things had been prepared and made ready for you. And in return for what do they obtain such things? For covering a roof, for a garment, for bread, for cold water, for visiting, for going into the prison.
>
> Saint John Chrysostom (AD 344–407) *Homily 79 on Matthew*

1. Explain the prediction of Jesus.

Matthew 24:1–2
CCC 585

2. For what should Christians be prepared?

Matthew 24:4–5
1 John 2:18

* Who comes to mind when you hear the term "antichrist?"

3. What can you learn from the following verses?

Matthew 24:6–8
Revelation 6:3, 8
Matthew 24:13
Revelation 2:7
CCC 161

4. What does Jesus foretell in Matthew 24:9–10?

5. Who is identified in these passages?

Daniel 12:10–11
Matthew 24:15
2 Thessalonians 2:3–10

6. What should believers do when they see the sacrilege? Matthew 24:16–20

7. What must happen before Christ comes again?

Matthew 24:14
Matthew 24:21–22
CCC 675

* How could the gospel be preached throughout the whole world?

8. Identify the warning in the following passages.

Matthew 24:23–26
1 John 2:18, 22; 2 John 7

9. Describe the *parousia*.

Matthew 24:29–31
1 Thessalonians 4:14–17
CCC 671, 672

10. How reliable is God's Word? Matthew 24:35

11. When will Jesus come again in glory? Matthew 24:36–43, CCC 673

12. What should you do until then? Matthew 24:43–50; 25:13

13. What is anticipated in Matthew 25:10? Revelation 19:7–9

14. Explain the moral of the Parable of the Talents. Matthew 25:14–29

15. Are everyone's talents the same? CCC 1936

* Share about specific talents YOU have and use for the kingdom of God.

16. Is hell real?

Matthew 25:30, 41
CCC 1034–1035

17. How could one avoid hell?

Matthew 25:34–36
CCC 1033, 1036

18. What will happen when Christ comes again?

Matthew 25:31–46
CCC 679
CCC 1038

19. What is a criterion for heaven? Matthew 25:40

20. What words would you like to hear at the end of your life? Matthew 25:34

* How prepared are you to meet the Lord and face judgment?

Chapter 20

The Last Supper
Matthew 26

Now as they were eating,
Jesus took bread, and blessed, and broke it, and gave it to the disciples
and said, "Take, eat; this is my body."
And he took a chalice, and when he had had given thanks
he gave it to them, saying,
"Drink of it, all of you, for this is my blood of the covenant,
which is poured out for many for the forgiveness of sins."
Matthew 26:26–28

Conspiracy to kill Jesus—*"You know that after two days the Passover is coming, and the Son of man will be delivered up to be crucified"* (Matthew 26:2). Jesus knows exactly what is unfolding, and alerts the apostles. Throughout His public ministry, the chief priests and elders have been hostile, trying to trap Jesus or to trip Him up in some way. They have failed. But, now they resort to any means necessary, even lying and violence, to get rid of Him. Caiaphas was the high priest in Jerusalem for almost twenty years, from AD 18—36. John's Gospel reports that Caiaphas had correctly prophesied the reason for Jesus' death. *"It is expedient for you that one man should die for the people"* (John 11:50). That is exactly what Jesus does. One man, Jesus Christ dies for the salvation of sinful humanity.

Anointing at Bethany—Simon the leper hosted a dinner at his home in Bethany. Obviously, Simon no longer has leprosy, or he would have been unclean, isolated, cast out from society, unable to socialize with others. Perhaps Simon is one of the lepers who had been healed by Jesus, but still carries his previous identity. An unnamed woman breaks an alabaster jar of costly ointment, probably spikenard from India, and anoints Jesus' head. Moses anointed the heads of Aaron and the Levitical priests with oil (Leviticus 8:12). And, the prophet Samuel anointed King David with oil (1 Samuel 16:13). So, this anonymous woman anoints Jesus, the high priest and King of Kings. Jesus accepts her kind gesture and indicates that this is a preparation for burial. The Catholic Church uses blessed oil to anoint the sick, which was formerly called "extreme unction" in preparation for death.

Women's work often goes unnoticed. Sometimes ladies perform acts that are overlooked and unappreciated. Homemakers prepare meals, wash clothes, clean homes, and raise children. Rarely does anyone notice. But, Jesus observes that this woman has lavished her love upon Him. She broke her expensive perfume bottle, and poured it *all* out for Him. She didn't offer Him a little and save the rest for herself. Jesus acknowledges that she has done a beautiful thing and will be remembered, wherever the gospel is preached. Jesus, a poor man, will be buried in a borrowed grave. She opened wide her hand to the poor (Deuteronomy 15:11; Proverbs 31:20).

Betrayal—In contrast to this unnamed woman's lavish display of worship and adoration, an act of treachery by one of Jesus' closest companions unfolds. Judas Iscariot, one of the Twelve, whether motivated by greed or disillusionment, goes to the chief priests and conspires to hand over Jesus to them. Caiaphas and the elders have already decided not to cause a riot during the feast, and give the Romans a reason to spill blood. Jerusalem's normal population of about 30,000 people swells with an additional 130,000 pilgrims for Passover. Extra Roman soldiers arrive to keep the peace, and they need very little provocation to exert force and resort to violence. But, Judas offers the chief priests an opportunity to arrest Jesus stealthily, helped by one of His very own intimates.

Judas, a weak negotiator, strikes a very poor bargain, agreeing to hand over Jesus for thirty pieces of silver. The King of Kings and Lord of Lords is betrayed by one of His closest disciples for the price of a slave! *If the ox gores a slave, male or female, the owner shall give to their master thirty shekels of silver* (Exodus 21:32). A good shepherd was paid thirty shekels of silver for his work, which he prophetically cast into the treasury in the house of the Lord (Zechariah 11:12–13).

Passover—an annual, weeklong celebration, recalling the Jews' exodus—God delivering them from slavery in Egypt—takes place every year, beginning on the fifteenth day of the month Nisan, which occurs in March or April. Homemakers remove all yeast and bread from their homes on the first day of Unleavened Bread, the fourteenth day of Nisan, which precedes the seven-day feast. Families gather together to enjoy a meal of a roasted, unblemished, yearling lamb, unleavened bread, and bitter herbs (Exodus 12:21–34). They recall God delivering them from their bondage, while the Egyptians suffered the death of their firstborn sons.

Usually, the Passover celebration includes women, children, relatives, and friends. But, on Jesus' last Passover with His disciples, He sits at table with the Twelve (Matthew 26:20), and announces, while they are eating that one of them will betray Him. The apostles are sorrowful. Who would betray Jesus? Fortunately, they each have the humility to recognize their human condition. Anyone is capable of treachery, but hopefully it is someone else. One after another, the apostles ask, *"Is it I, Lord?"* (Matthew 26:22). Eleven loyal apostles address Jesus as *"Lord,"* the one to whom they have given their lives and allegiance. Judas, however, addresses Jesus as rabbi, or teacher, indicating someone more distant.

The Last Supper—Artists often depict this scene, in which Jesus reclines at table with His twelve apostles. Usually, the beloved disciple John appears beardless to indicate his youth. Peter prominently sits on the other side of Jesus. Judas may be heading toward the door for his escape. Others may be more difficult to identify. But, artists have enabled believers to fix clearly in the mind's eye this important event. Even some Catholic churches are named "Blessed Sacrament" to underscore the importance of the amazing liturgical events taking place at the Last Supper of Jesus' life. Catholics remember and celebrate this event every Holy Thursday, thanking God for the gifts of the priesthood and the Eucharist.

Throughout Jesus' ministry, the apostles have observed the power of Jesus' *words*. Jesus speaks and incredible things happen—a storm at sea ceases, winds calm down, sins are forgiven, and people are cured of incurable diseases. Sometimes Jesus touches the sick. Other times He just speaks and miracles happen. Tonight at this Last Supper, Jesus' *words* work another miracle before their very eyes, a miracle that will be repeated in Catholic churches daily over the centuries.

Now as they were eating, Jesus took bread, and blessed, and broke it, and gave it to the disciples and said, "Take, eat; this is my body." And he took a chalice, and when he had had given thanks he gave it to them, saying, "Drink of it, all of you, for this is my blood of the covenant, which is poured out for many for the forgiveness of sins" (Matthew 26:26–28). Jesus identifies the bread and wine with His Body and Blood, which will be sacrificed on the Cross. Jesus, high priest and king, fulfills the promise of God. *As for you also, because of the blood of my covenant with you, I will set your captives free from the waterless pit* (Zechariah 9:11). *"Behold, the days are coming, says the LORD, when I will make a new covenant with the house of Israel and the house of Judah. . . . I will be their God, and they shall be my people. . . . I will forgive their iniquity, and I will remember their sin no more"* (Jeremiah 31:31, 33, 34).

Jesus institutes the Eucharist (the fifth Luminous Mystery of the Rosary), linking this sacred mystery with His sacrifice on the Cross, and anticipating the Marriage Supper of the Lamb in the New Jerusalem—the messianic banquet that had been foretold (Isaiah 25:6): *"Blessed are those who are invited to the marriage supper of the Lamb"* (Revelation 19:9). Catholics recognize the Blessed Sacrament as the source and summit of the Christian life, the source of divine grace, since it communicates Christ's divine life to the believing recipient. Christ Himself, living and glorious is present in the Eucharist—body, blood, soul, and divinity in a true, real, and substantial manner.

The Body is truly united to divinity, the Body, which was from that of the Holy Virgin . . . through the Holy Spirit, just as it was through the Holy Spirit that the Lord took on Himself from the Holy Mother of God the flesh that subsisted in Himself. More than this we do not know, except that the word of God is true and effective and all-powerful, but the manner [of transubstantiation] is inscrutable . . .

For those who partake worthily and with faith, it is for the remission of sins and for life everlasting, and a safeguard to soul and body. . . . The Bread and the Wine are *not a type* of the Body and Blood of Christ—perish the thought—but the deified Body Itself of the Lord, since the Lord Himself has said: *"This is My Body."* He did not say a type of His Body, but His Body; nor a type of His Blood, but His Blood.

Saint John Damascene (AD 645–749), *The Source of Knowledge*, 3, 13

> The food that you receive, that *living bread which came down from heaven,* supplies the very substance of eternal life, and whoever will eat it will never die, for it is the body of Christ. Consider now which is the more excellent: the bread of angels or the flesh of Christ, which is indeed the body that gives life.
>
> Saint Ambrose (AD 340–397), *On the Mysteries,* 1–7

> He did not say, "This is the symbol of My Body, and this, of My Blood," but, "This is My Body and My Blood," teaching us not to look upon the nature of what is before us, but that it is transformed by means of the Eucharistic action into Flesh and Blood.
>
> Theodor of Mopsuestia [†AD 428], *Commentary on Matthew,* 26:26

Jesus predicts Peter's denial. In this twenty-sixth chapter of Matthew, Jesus makes three prophecies, foretelling events that will take place in the immediate future. Each of them unfolds exactly as Jesus says.

1) *"You know that after two days the Passover is coming, and the Son of man will be delivered up to be crucified"* (Matthew 26:2).
2) *And as they were eating, he said, "Truly, I say to you, one of you will betray me"* (Matthew 26:21).
3) *Jesus said to him [Peter], "Truly, I say to you, this very night, before the cock crows, you will deny me three times"* (Matthew 26:34).

Peter's denial occurs later that evening, in the courtyard of the high priest. Just as Jesus foretold, Peter denies Our Lord three times, once with an oath and then with swearing. When the cock crows, Peter remembers what Jesus had foretold. Peter's conscience awakens and remorse for his cowardice moves him to weep with shame and a repentant heart (Matthew 26:69–75). Peter shows the remorse that we all should feel for our sins.

The Agony in the Garden—After singing the last hymn of Passover, probably one of the closing Hallel Psalms (Psalm 115–118), Jesus and the remaining apostles go to the Mount of Olives to the Garden of Gethsemane, meaning "oil press." Jesus asks the apostles to sit and wait, while He goes to pray. Peter, James and John, the sons of Zebedee, continue with Jesus to wait and pray. These three apostles seem to be the closest to Jesus, since they are privileged to witness three major events.

+ Restoring a dead girl to life—*He permitted no one to enter with him, except Peter and John and James, and the father and mother of the child . . . But taking her by the hand he called, saying "Child, arise." And her spirit returned, and she got up at once* (Luke 8:51–55).
+ The Transfiguration—*Jesus took with him Peter and James and John his brother, and led them up a high mountain apart. And he was transfigured before them, and his face shone like the sun* (Matthew 17:1–2).
+ Agony in the Garden—*And taking with him Peter and the two sons of Zebedee, he began to be sorrowful and troubled. He said to them, "My soul is very sorrowful, even to death; remain here, and watch with me"* (Matthew 26:37–38).

Whether from the wine of the Passover meal, the exhaustion of the day, or the anxiety of the predicted Passion of the Lord, the apostles fail. They cannot stay awake, watch, and pray one hour with Jesus. He prays in agony alone. By the same measure, how much time do you spend in prayer with Jesus each day? Could you stay awake a bit longer, and watch with Him?

"Our Father" (Matthew 6:9)	*"My Father, if it be possible, let this chalice pass from me* (Matthew 26:39)
"Thy will be done" (Matthew 6:10)	*nevertheless, not as I will, but as you will. . . . My Father, if this cannot pass unless I drink it, your will be done"* (Matthew 26:39b, 42)

Jesus' prayer, as previously taught to the disciples, gives total submission to the perfect will and plan of God the Father. As a man, Jesus knows that He will experience unimaginable pain and suffering. Physically, He will be scourged and crucified. Spiritually, He will bear the sins of the world, which impinges upon His perfect unity with the Father. Jesus, freely and willingly hands Himself over.

The betrayal, arrest, and trial of Jesus—As Jesus had foretold in Matthew 26:21 at the Last Supper, one of the Twelve betrays Him. *Even my bosom friend in whom I trusted, who ate of my bread, has lifted his heel against me* (Psalm 41:9). Judas Iscariot betrays Jesus with a kiss, the traditional gesture of love and affection. Jesus had also predicted denial and desertion. *Then all the disciples deserted him and fled* (Matthew 26:56). Jesus is abandoned in His time of need.

The Sanhedrin was made up of seventy-one Jewish elders. Probably, they were not all present for the travesty of justice perpetrated against Jesus. *Now the chief priests and the whole council sought false testimony against Jesus that they might put him to death* (Matthew 26:59), in direct opposition to Mosaic Law. *You shall not bear false witness against your neighbor* (Exodus 20:16). The death penalty requires the corroborating evidence of two witnesses (Deuteronomy 17:6). False witnesses bring charges of blasphemy against Jesus, who remains silent. *He was oppressed, and he was afflicted, yet he opened not his mouth* (Isaiah 53:7).

Caiaphas, the high priest forces Jesus to respond by invoking an oath, *"I adjure you by the living God, tell us if you are the Christ, the Son of God"* (Matthew 26:63). Jesus responds by forcing the accuser to accept responsibility for the assertion, without self-incrimination. *"You have said so. But I tell you, hereafter you will see the Son of man seated at the right hand of Power, and coming on the clouds of heaven"* (Matthew 26:64). The Prophet Daniel had foretold, *behold, with the clouds of heaven there came one like a son of man, and he came to the Ancient of Days and was presented before him* (Daniel 7:13).

Caiaphas wrongly judges that Jesus has blasphemed and condemns Him to death. According to Mosaic Law, blasphemy deserves death by stoning. *"He who blasphemes the name of the Lord shall be put to death; all the congregation shall stone him"* (Leviticus 24:16). Even if Jesus had committed this crime, which He didn't, because He *is* God, the high priest does not follow Mosaic Law. Nothing in Mosaic Law warrants crucifixion! Caiaphas further breaks the Law by tearing his priestly robe: *"The priest who is chief among his brethren shall not tear his clothes* (Leviticus 21:10). The religious leaders then mock, humiliate, and abuse Jesus, fulfilling the prophecies of the Suffering Servant in Isaiah 50:6, 53:3–5.

The apostles celebrate the Last Supper with Jesus, and then desert Him. Similar things happen today. Some Catholics receive Holy Communion and then race out of the church, without pausing to give thanks, or finish the liturgy. Others betray Jesus by sinful double lives. Catholics deny Jesus, when they fail to stand up for Christian moral principles. Sadly, some believers desert Jesus, when the Gospel conflicts with popular opinion or their convenience. Who will stand with Jesus?

1. What time did Jesus choose to provide a spectacular gift?

Matthew 26:1–2,17–18
CCC 1339

2. What did Jesus foretell in Matthew 26:1–2?

3. What were the chief priests and elders planning? Matthew 26:3–5

4. Explain the drama in Matthew 26:6–13.

* How does Jesus evaluate the woman's action? Matthew 26:10–13

5. Who betrays Jesus? Does Jesus anticipate this?

Psalm 41:9
Matthew 26:14–16
Matthew 26:20–25

6. Compare these accounts.

Matthew 26:26–29	Mark 14:22–25	Luke 22:19–20	1 Corinthians 11:23ff

7. Use the Catechism to explain this event.

CCC 610, 613
CCC 1328–31
CCC 1365

* Recall your First Holy Communion. What does the Eucharist mean to you now?

8. What does Jesus anticipate?

Matthew 26:29
CCC 1403

* Have you ever been betrayed by someone?

** Have you ever betrayed someone you love?

9. What prophecy does Jesus recall? How is it fulfilled?

Zechariah 13:7
Matthew 26:30–35
Matthew 26:69–75

10. What does Peter's denial reveal about Jesus?

CCC 1429
CCC 1851

*** Define Peter's sin. CCC 2092

11. Where does Jesus go after the Last Supper? Matthew 26:36–38

12. Jesus takes which three apostles with Him, and why? Matthew 26:37–38

13. For what does Jesus pray?

Matthew 26:39, 42
Hebrews 5:7–8
CCC 609
CCC 612

* For what do you pray?

14. What did Jesus ask the apostles? What does this teach us?

Matthew 26:38, 41
CCC 2719
CCC 2733
CCC 2849

15. By what gesture was Jesus betrayed? Matthew 26:47–49

16. How does Jesus address the betrayer? Matthew 26:50

17. What does Jesus command?

Matthew 26:51–53
CCC 2261

18. What did the disciples do? Matthew 26:56

19. Describe the accusations against Jesus and the religious authorities.

Matthew 26:57–62
Matthew 26:65–67
CCC 596–598

20. What does Jesus reveal? Matthew 26:63–64

CHAPTER 21

Passion Narrative
Matthew 27

And over his head they put the charge against him,
which read, "This is Jesus the King of the Jews."
Matthew 27:37

Jesus is condemned to death. Matthew knew that Mosaic courts could not meet during the night. The behavior of the temple authorities, interrogating Jesus through the night and legally convening the Sanhedrin only at sunrise was scandalous. Obtaining a quorum was difficult, due to the festival. Many members were certainly irritated at being called away from their families and from their synagogues. The chief priests contrive to have Jesus put to death, which they had been trying to do all along. When Jesus healed a man's withered hand on the sabbath, *the Pharisees went out and took counsel against him, how to destroy him* (Matthew 12:14). Now the chief priests and elders *took counsel* again to put Jesus to death, binding an innocent man to deliver over to Pilate, just as Jesus foretold.

Judas despairs. Perhaps the indignity Jesus suffers, and the death sentence shock Judas. Peter also betrays Jesus, but repents, and is restored. Judas regrets his sin, *"I have sinned in betraying innocent blood"* (Matthew 27:4), but attempts to undo his treachery by returning the money. Often people try to undo sins committed, or fix wrongs that only God can repair. Judas throws the thirty pieces of silver *into the treasury in the house of the Lord* (Zechariah 11:13), just as the Lord's shepherd had done. The money came from the temple treasury in the first place. The chief priests paid Judas and liars to hand over and falsely accuse Jesus. They continue to be blind to their own sins. So, they buy the "potter's field," called the Field of Blood, a stretch of land stripped of topsoil, and mined for clay and lime for use in making pottery. Such land could not be used for agriculture, but was purchased for use as a cemetery, fitting in view of the fact that it was bought with blood money.

Sacred Scripture records two different accounts of Judas' death. Matthew reports: *And throwing down the pieces of silver in the temple, he departed; and he went and hanged himself* (Matthew 27:5). Luke, in the Acts of the Apostles, reports Peter saying: *Now this man [Judas] bought a field with the reward of his wickedness; and falling headlong he burst open in the middle and all his bowels gushed out* (Acts 1:18). In antiquity, it would be plausible to hang oneself from the branch of a tree. If the branch subsequently broke from the weight of the body, the plummet could result in abdominal evisceration. So, both accounts can be true. In any event, Judas came to a horrible end.

Pontius Pilate—Every Sunday in Mass around the world, a billion Catholics recall this notorious man, while reciting the Nicene Creed. "For our sake He was crucified under Pontius Pilate, He suffered death and was buried." Pontius Pilate, known for his cruelty and disdain for Judaism, governed Judea from AD 26–36. He extorted money from the temple treasury to build a water system, and massacred Galilean Jews, while they were offering sacrifices in the temple. Two thousand years later, this legacy of Pontius Pilate endures from his cowardly act, in authorizing the innocent Jesus Christ of Nazareth to suffer an excruciating Passion and death. He leaves quite a treacherous legacy in his wake!

Despite his horrible history, Pilate does ask a few excellent questions for posterity. *"Are you the King of the Jews?"* (Matthew 27:11). Jesus' response indicates that Pilate has answered his own question. Pilate orders that this true inscription be placed above the cross of Christ, *"This is Jesus the King of the Jews"* (Matthew 27:37), in Hebrew, Latin, and Greek, despite the chief priests' protests. Pilate, gazing at perfect Goodness and absolute Truth, asks: *"What is truth?"* (John 18:38). Jesus had already revealed to His followers, *"I am the way, and the truth, and the life; no one comes to the Father, but by me"* (John 14:6). But, Pilate, like so many others, refuses to see the truth and accept the way and the life.

Dreams emerge repeatedly in Matthew's Gospel. The Lord appears to Joseph in a dream to explain the birth of Jesus (Matthew 1:20). Dreams warn the wise men not to return to Herod (Matthew 2:12), and a dream warns Joseph to flee to Egypt with Mary and Jesus (Matthew 2:13). Now Pilate's wife, troubled by a dream, warns him to *"have nothing to do with that righteous man"* (Matthew 27:19). Women in the first century had no legal standing, and could not testify in a trial. A woman's word meant nothing. Nevertheless, a non-Jewish woman receives a dream and learns that Jesus of Nazareth is "a righteous man." Pilate receives a warning from his wife that he chooses to ignore. People often fail to heed warnings to their own peril.

Knowing that Jesus is innocent, but accused due to envy, Pilate decides to free Him through a Passover amnesty. Pilate offers the people an easy choice: release the notorious murderer and insurrectionist Barabbas, or the innocent Jesus Christ. Surprisingly, the crowds are incited to choose the release of a murderer, and demand the most humiliating and painful form of Roman execution imaginable for Jesus. Barabbas, whose name *bar abba* means "son of the father" receives pardon, while Jesus of Nazareth, the "true Son of God the Father" receives an undeserved death sentence. Only one person was genuinely happy that day—the robber Barabbas. Jesus died for him, in his place, and for the remission of his sins.

Tradition says that the Apostle Matthew eventually would give his life for Christ, after writing about what Christ did for him. The mystery of the crucifixion continues for suffering Christians down through history, in the Roman Empire for the first three centuries, in Muslim Spain in the 800s, in Japan and France in the 1700s, in Armenia and Iran in the 1910s, in Mexico and Russia in the 1920s, in Spain in the 1930s, in Germany and occupied lands in the 1940s, and today in Syria and Iraq. The list could go on, for hardly any land is without its martyrs.

Victims are not just statistics, but real people who find themselves called to give witness. In 1941, at Auschwitz concentration camp in occupied Poland, Prisoner 16670, a Catholic priest, volunteered to die in the place of Prisoner 5659, a married man with children. The layman,

Franciszek Gajowniczek, survived and was present at the Vatican for the beatification of Father Maximilian Maria Kolbe in 1971 by Blessed Paul VI, and again for his canonization in 1982 by Saint John Paul II. Both of these men lived the reality of the Cross.

Pilate knows that Jesus is innocent. Luke reports Pilate saying three times, *"I find no crime in this man"* (Luke 23:4, 14, 22). Pilate cares not for true justice, but panders to the riotous mob. Despite ignoring his wife's warning, Pilate parrots her description of Jesus as a righteous man. *"I am innocent of this righteous man's blood"* (Matthew 27:24). Pilate's hand-washing ritual was not a common Roman practice, but speaks clearly to the Jews. *I wash my hands in innocence, and go about your altar, O Lord* (Psalm 26:6). Pilate confirms Jesus' innocence and righteousness, by word and action. Pilate's claim of his own innocence in Jesus' condemnation contrasts with the people's acceptance of responsibility.

The prophet Jeremiah, an innocent man, warned the people: *"Only know for certain that if you put me to death, you will bring innocent blood upon yourselves and upon this city"* (Jeremiah 26:15). Those who demand crucifixion for Jesus, accept a blood curse upon themselves and their descendants. Judas, Pilate, the chief priests, and every sinner in history bears guilt for the suffering and death of Jesus.

> "I came down from heaven to save you. I took your sorrows upon Me; I had no need to do so, but My love for you drew Me on. The lesson I wanted you to learn was that of patience, of bearing the sorrows of life without bitterness. From the hour of My birth until My death upon the cross, there was never a moment when I had no sorrow to bear. My store of worldly goods amounted to very little; many and frequent were the complaints I heard people make about Me; when they shamed and insulted Me I took it gently. My kindnesses were repaid with ingratitude, My miracles with blasphemy, My teachings with rebuke."
>
> Thomas à Kempis, *The Imitation of Christ*,
> (San Francisco, CA: Ignatius Press, 2005), 137

The Suffering Servant—was prophesied by the prophet Isaiah and the Psalmist. The Messiah would be a suffering servant, taking on the sins of the world, not a military hero or political leader, as some hoped and expected.

✝ *All who see me mock at me, they make mouths at me, they wag their heads* (Psalm 22:7).
✝ *I gave my back to those who struck me, and my cheeks to those who pulled out the beard; I hid not my face from shame and spitting* (Isaiah 50:6).
✝ *I can count all my bones—they stare and gloat over me; they divide my garments among them, and for my clothing they cast lots* (Psalm 22:17–18).
✝ *But he was wounded for our transgressions, he was bruised for our iniquities; upon him was the chastisement that made us whole, and with his stripes we are healed* (Isaiah 53:5).

Plaiting a crown of thorns they put it on his head, and put a reed in his right hand. And kneeling before him they mocked him, saying, "Hail, King of the Jews!" (Matthew 27:29). The crowning with thorns appears in three Gospels (Matthew 27:29; Mark 15:17; John 19:2, 5). Thorns formed part of the curse of Adam after the Fall in the Garden of Eden (Genesis 3:18), and this crowning signifies Jesus taking that curse upon Himself. The previous night, Jesus was cruelly mocked, struck, and spat upon in the presence of the chief priests and elders. Now soldiers strip Jesus and put one of their scarlet military robes on Him, with a reed, similar to a royal scepter. They kneel and mock Him, saying, *"Hail, King of the Jews!"* (Matthew 27:29).

Pilate places the soldier's words on the Cross. These Romans get it wrong, however. The true title of the Messiah is not "King of the Jews" but "King of Israel," as pronounced by the crowd (Matthew 27:42). In the Old Testament, "Jew" means a member of the tribe of Judah, and in the New Testament an inhabitant of Judea. The term "Israel," however, incorporates all the people, of all twelve tribes, wherever they may live. Several groups of people mock Jesus—chief priests, elders, soldiers, passers-by, and the robbers crucified with Him (Matthew 26:67; 27:30; 27:39–44). But the mocking doesn't end with Jesus' crucifixion. Even today, God is mocked and blasphemed in casual conversation, music, entertainment, and books.

As they were marching out, they came upon a man of Cyrene, Simon by name; this man they compelled to carry his cross (Matthew 27:32). Matthew does not give as much information about this man as the other evangelists, who say that Simon was coming in from the fields. Each morning farmers, then and now, brought fresh produce from garden plots to sell in the markets of Jerusalem. After delivering his goods to the marketplace, Simon of Cyrene was now the right man, in the right place, at the right time, to help Jesus.

They came to a place called Golgotha (which means the place of a skull) (Matthew 27:33). The holiest of Christian holy places is the site of the crucifixion, death, burial, and Resurrection of Jesus. The Hebrew name *Gulgôlet* "skull," transformed into Aramaic by locals as *Gûlgaltâ* "the skull," translated into Greek by the evangelists as *Kraniou Topos* "place of a cranium," and into Latin by Saint Jerome as *Calvariae Locus* "place of the bald pate." Golgotha and Calvary are one and the same, the word for skull in Aramaic and in Latin. The shape of the hill suggested the name, and gave rise to legends that the skull of Adam was buried there.

Jesus dies on the cross. Matthew does not describe many details of Jesus' actual suffering on the cross, but rather highlights the events that are happening all around Him. Darkness covers the land. *Now from the sixth hour there was darkness over all the land until the ninth hour* (Matthew 27:45). The sixth hour is noon; the ninth hour is halfway between noon and twilight, a shorter time in winter than in summer. The Crucifixion in the Spring Equinox, when the hours of day equal the hours of night, provided three full hours of light, from noon until three in the afternoon. Darkness engulfed Egypt, in the last plague before the angel of death struck the land, but passed over the Hebrews, who had sprinkled the lamb's blood on the doorposts of their houses. The noontime darkness on Good Friday indicates that the Passover of the Lamb is about to take place; death now will be deprived of power, because of the Blood of the Lamb absorbed by the arms of the Cross.

In His agony, Jesus prays a psalm of great anguish, a plea to the Father for deliverance from suffering. Psalm 22 begins: *My God, my God, why have you forsaken me?* (Matthew 27:46). Apparently, some bystanders recognize the psalm, when they say, *"He trusts in God; let God deliver him now"* (Matthew 27:43). The psalm continues: *"He committed his cause to the Lord; let him deliver him, let him rescue him, for he delights in him!"* (Psalm 22:8).

It is not in abandoning the Cross, that Jesus redeems sinful humanity, but in embracing the Cross. Jesus willingly accepts the humiliation and pain of crucifixion precisely to atone for all the sins of the world. Jesus may have been too exhausted to finish praying the psalm, but the last verses of the psalm are telling. *Posterity shall serve him; men shall tell of the Lord to the coming generation, and proclaim his deliverance to a people yet unborn, that he has wrought it* (Psalm 22:30–31). We are those who were yet unborn, but rejoice now in proclaiming that Jesus has conquered sin and death, and by His Cross He has redeemed the world. I adore you, O Christ, because by Your Cross You redeemed me.

"Eli, Eli, la'ma sabach'-tha'ni?" that is, "My God, my God, why have you forsaken me?" (Matthew 27:46). Matthew relates the first words in Hebrew—*"Eli, Eli"*—but Mark puts them in an Aramaic targum, or translation—*"E'lo-i, Elo-i"* (Mark 15:34). Jesus himself may have spoken in both languages, first in Hebrew, then in Aramaic, as is the practice for readings from the Hebrew Bible in the synagogue, then and now. In Jesus' time, only the original Hebrew was allowed in book form, but the lector was expected to give an Aramaic translation immediately after the Hebrew, verse-by-verse for the Torah, and three verses at a time for the Prophets.

And Jesus cried again with a loud voice and yielded up his spirit. And behold, the curtain of the temple was torn in two (Matthew 27:50–51a). The splitting of the sacred veil of the temple, marking the boundary between divine and human space, accompanied the separation of the sacred human soul of Jesus from His sacred human body. The divine nature neither suffered nor died, but the sacred person of Jesus did. The Council of Ephesus decreed that "God was born of the Virgin Mary" and that "God died on the Cross." Though the divine nature remained unchanged, the divine Second Person of the Blessed Trinity truly experienced these things.

The temple curtain split in two symbolizes a new era in salvation history. The old sacrificial system ends. Jesus, the unblemished Lamb of God, takes away the sins of the world, by His one perfect sacrifice, acceptable to God the Father. The Letter to the Hebrews explains that Jesus is the perfect High Priest of the New Covenant. *But when Christ appeared as a high priest of the good things that have come . . . he entered once for all into the Holy Place, taking not the blood of goats and calves but his own blood, thus securing eternal redemption* (Hebrews 9:11–12).

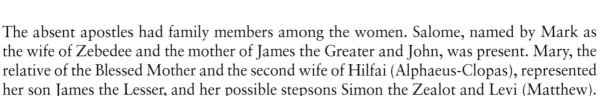

The absent apostles had family members among the women. Salome, named by Mark as the wife of Zebedee and the mother of James the Greater and John, was present. Mary, the relative of the Blessed Mother and the second wife of Hilfai (Alphaeus-Clopas), represented her son James the Lesser, and her possible stepsons Simon the Zealot and Levi (Matthew). As many as five of the apostles, then, had mothers or stepmothers among the mourning women. These were the major sources of information for the Passion Narratives of Mark and of Matthew.

Of the evangelists, only Matthew reports the amazing events following the death of Jesus and the tearing of the temple curtain: *the earth shook, and the rocks were split; the tombs also were opened, and many bodies of the saints who had fallen asleep were raised, and coming out of the tombs after his resurrection they went into the holy city and appeared to many* (Matthew 27:51–53). One wonders about the identity of these deceased saints, and where they went after their walk in the holy city. They will come again *at the coming of our Lord Jesus with all his saints* (1 Thessalonians 3:13), to participate in the general judgment.

Finally, the centurion makes the same profession of faith as the apostles did earlier, when Jesus walked on the Sea of Galilee: *"Truly you are [this was] the Son of God!"* (Matthew 14:33; 27:54). The chief priests and elders see the same suffering that the centurion sees, but refuse to believe. They know Psalm 22 and Isaiah's prophecies, but close their minds to Jesus. Many women, faithful disciples of Jesus along the way, remain with Him. True, faithful love perseveres to the bitter end.

The burial of Jesus—Joseph of Arimatheá, a wealthy man, had been a member of the Sanhedrin. It is unclear whether Joseph participated in the late night interrogation of Jesus, but it is doubtful. Luke reports that Joseph was *a good and righteous man, who had not consented to their purpose and deed, and he was looking for the kingdom of God* (Luke 23:50–51). As a disciple of Jesus, Joseph was probably not invited to the meeting. Mosaic Law required that a criminal, punished by death, must be buried that same day (Deuteronomy 21:22–23).

And Joseph took the body, and wrapped it in a clean linen shroud, and laid it in his own new tomb, which he had hewn in the rock; and he rolled a great stone to the door of the tomb, and departed (Matthew 27:59–60). Joseph of Arimatheá had a new tomb that he had excavated for himself, and obtained permission to place the body of Jesus there, rather than in the common grave where many of the corpses were consigned. So, the place of crucifixion and the place of burial are only a few steps apart, and both lie within a single basilica, called the Holy Sepulcher (Tomb) by Roman Catholics, but called the Anastasis (Resurrection) by Byzantines.

The Holy Sacrifice of the Mass always and everywhere encompasses the mysteries of the death and Resurrection of Christ, and especially here where the events took place. Catholic Priests who visit Jerusalem may offer Mass both inside the tomb itself and nearby at the anointing stone, where Joseph washed and wrapped the Body. The Shroud of Turin is viewed by millions of pilgrims. The Shroud gives evidence of both the Passion and the Resurrection, because it bears bloodstains from wounds left by the whip, the spear, and the nails, while also containing a negative image on both front and back as if left by a powerful display of radiant energy.

Joseph's great respect and care for the corpse of Jesus provides an example for Christian burial practices, which show respect for the dignity of the human body. Jesus, born in poverty in a manger, dies as a poor man, laid in a borrowed tomb. Joseph provides further evidence of the death of Jesus. As he wraps Jesus in a linen shroud, Joseph of Arimatheá can feel the dead weight of the lifeless body.

The guards at the tomb—The following day is the sabbath. The chief priests and Pharisees, oppose one another on most matters, but like Pilate and Herod, agree in the condemnation of Jesus. They remember the words of Jesus. While still alive, Jesus prophesied, *"After three days I will rise again"* (Matthew 16:21; 17:23; 20:19; 27:63). They want Pilate to secure the tomb. Pilate sends soldiers to guard the tomb, but makes them secure it themselves. So, the chief priests, who criticized Jesus for working miracles on the sabbath, go to work to seal the tomb on the sabbath!

The crucifixion and death of Jesus of Nazareth on a Friday afternoon, probably in April of the year around AD 30–33, was the most sorrowful Friday of all time. The apostles hide in fear. Mary, the Mother of Jesus, and other women mourn. Do the women remember what Jesus told them would happen on the third day?

The mystery of Christ's suffering, death and Resurrection inspires us to go on in hope—times of trouble and testing, when endured with Christ, with faith in Him, already contain the light of the Resurrection, the new life of a world reborn, the passover of all those who believe in His word.

In that crucified Man who is the Son of God, even death itself takes on new meaning and purpose: it is redeemed and overcome, it becomes a passage to new life. *"Unless a grain of wheat falls into the earth and dies, it remains just a single grain; but if it dies, it produces much fruit"* (John 12:24). Let us entrust ourselves to the Mother of Christ. May Mary, who accompanied her Son along His way of sorrows, who stood beneath the cross at the hour of His death, and who inspired the Church at its birth to live in God's presence, lead our hearts and the hearts of every family through the vast *mysterium passionis* towards the *mysterium paschale*, towards that light which breaks forth from Christ's Resurrection and reveals the definitive victory of love, joy and life over evil, suffering and death. Amen.

Pope Benedict XVI, *Good Friday Address*, April 6, 2002

1. What happened to Jesus in Matthew 27:1–2?

2. Compare the following accounts.

Matthew 27:3–10
Acts 1:16–20

3. What questions does Pilate ask Jesus?

Matthew 27:11
Matthew 27:13
John 18:37
John 18:38

4. Use a dictionary and the Catechism to define "truth." CCC 2468

5. Explain the drama in Matthew 27:15–23.

6. Compare the following passages. Who is responsible for Jesus' death?

Matthew 27:25
Acts 5:28
CCC 597–598

7. How did the soldiers treat Jesus? Matthew 27:27–31

8. Who helped Jesus? Matthew 27:32

9. Compare the following verses. What prophecy does Jesus fulfill?

Psalm 22:18
Matthew 27:35

10. How is Jesus identified? By whom?

Matthew 27:29
Matthew 27:37
Matthew 27:42

* By what titles would you identify Jesus?

11. What did Jesus foretell?

Matthew 26:61
John 2:19
Acts 6:14

12. How did Jesus feel about the temple?

CCC 585
CCC 586

13. What did Jesus pray on the Cross? How does Psalm 22 end?

Matthew 27:46
Psalm 22:1
Psalm 22:30–31

* What comfort or encouragement does this offer to you?

14. What did the signs of Jesus' life show?

Matthew 27:42–43
CCC 515

15. What does the tearing of the Temple curtain indicate?

Matthew 27:51
Hebrews 10:19–22

16. What happened immediately after Jesus died? Matthew 27:51–53

17. What can you learn about the abode of the dead? CCC 632–635

18. What did the centurion proclaim? Matthew 27:54

19. Who buried Jesus? Who watched these events? Matthew 27:55–61

20. Describe the drama in Matthew 27:62–65.

CHAPTER 22

The Resurrection
Matthew 28

*"Go therefore and make disciples of all nations,
baptizing them in the name of the Father and of the Son and of the Holy Spirit,
teaching them to observe all that I have commanded you;
and behold, I am with you always, to the close of the age."*
Matthew 28:19–20

The most spectacular event in all of human history—took place during the middle of the night or early morning on the first Easter Sunday, and nobody witnessed it. Many people were eyewitnesses of the soldiers scourging and crucifying Jesus. His mother Mary, apostle John, and Mary Magdalene stood at the foot of the cross, watching Him suffer, until He breathed His last. When Jesus died, darkness covered the land, the earth quaked, and a centurion said, *"Truly this was the Son of God!"* (Matthew 27:54). Women watched the dead body of Jesus being placed in Joseph of Arimatheá's new tomb. A rock secured the opening to the tomb, which soldiers guarded. But, then what happened on the third day?

This luminous event, on which all of human history hinges, occurs in the pre-dawn darkness before no human eyewitnesses. Jesus conquers sin and death. He returns from the domain of the shadow of death with a glorified body. Jesus alive, not simply a resuscitated corpse, returns from death in a new form—a glorified body.

When women go to the tomb at dawn on the first day of the week, there is another great earthquake (Matthew 27:51–54; 28:2). An angel of the Lord rolls back the stone from the mouth of the tomb, and tells the women: *"Do not be afraid; for I know that you seek Jesus who was crucified. He is not here; for he has risen as he said"* (Matthew 28:5–6). The angel appears luminescent, like lightening in snow-white clothes. Terrified, the guards faint. The angel sitting on the stone, which had blocked the tomb symbolizes Christ's victory over death. Like Mary's virginal conception of Jesus, this sign marks a great invisible reality. The angel tells the women that Jesus will meet the disciples in Galilee, where His mission originated. As they leave, in fear and joy, emotions that most people experience during their lifetime, they meet Jesus! They hold His feet and worship Him. Jesus is not a ghost. He has a resurrected, glorified body that they touch.

Jesus repeats the words of the angel. *"Do not be afraid; go and tell my brethren to go to Galilee, and there they will see me"* (Matthew 28:10). Jesus calls His apostles *brethren* or "brothers," indicating that He has forgiven their cowardice. Jesus commissions the women to bring the good news to the apostles, making the women the "apostles to the apostles." The women see Jesus with their eyes, touch Him with their hands, and with their ears hear His voice speak to them.

"If Christ has not been raised, then our preaching is in vain and your faith is in vain. We are even found to be misrepresenting God, because we testified of God that he raised Christ" (1 Corinthians 15:14–15). With these words Saint Paul explains quite drastically what faith in the Resurrection of Jesus Christ means for the Christian message over all: it is its very foundation. The Christian faith stands or falls with the trust of the testimony that Christ is risen from the dead . . .

Only if Jesus is risen has anything really new occurred that changes the world and the situation of mankind. Then he becomes the criterion on which we can rely. For then God has truly revealed himself. To this extent, in our quest for the figure of Jesus, the Resurrection is the crucial point. Whether Jesus merely *was* or whether he also *is*—this depends on the Resurrection . . .

Jesus' Resurrection was about breaking out into an entirely new form of life, into a life that is no longer subject to the law of dying and becoming, but lies beyond it—a life that opens up a new dimension of human existence. . . . In Jesus' Resurrection a new possibility of human existence is attained that affects everyone and that opens up a future, a new kind of future, for mankind . . .

Jesus has not returned to a normal human life in this world like Lazarus and the others whom Jesus raised from the dead. He has entered upon a different life—he has entered the vast breadth of God himself, and it is from there that he reveals himself to his followers.

For the disciples, too, this was something utterly unexpected, to which they were only slowly able to adjust. Jewish faith did indeed know of a resurrection of the dead at the end of time. New life was linked to the inbreaking of a new world and thus made complete sense. If there is a new world, then there is also a new mode of life there. But a resurrection into definitive otherness in the midst of the continuing old world was not foreseen and therefore at first made no sense. So the promise of resurrection remained initially unintelligible to the disciples.

. . . for the disciples the Resurrection was just as real as the Cross. It presupposes that they were simply overwhelmed by the reality, that, after their initial hesitation and astonishment, they could no longer ignore the reality. It is truly he. He is alive; he has spoken to us; he allowed us to touch him, even if he no longer belongs to the realm of the tangible in the normal way.

The paradox was indescribable. He was quite different, no mere resuscitated corpse, but one living anew and forever in the power of God.

Pope Benedict XVI, *Jesus of Nazareth: Holy Week,*
(San Francisco: Ignatius Press, 2011), 241–246

Who witnessed the Resurrection of Jesus? Who observed the virginal conception of Jesus in the Blessed Virgin? Only God the Father, Jesus, and the Holy Spirit are privileged to witness and participate in these miraculous events. Humans are only allowed to observe the results, or are informed about these mysteries. Yet, God provides ample evidence to testify to the bodily Resurrection of Jesus of Nazareth. Consider Jesus' many post-Resurrection appearances to His disciples and friends.

After His Resurrection, Jesus appears to:

Mary Magdalene and other women
    (Matthew 28:8–10; Mark 16:9; John 20:11–18),
Simon Peter (Luke 24:34; John 21:7ff),
Ten apostles, excluding Thomas (Luke 24:36–43; John 20:19–25),
All eleven apostles, including Thomas (Mark 16:14; John 20:26–29),
Disciples on the road to Emmaus (Mark 16:12; Luke 24:13–25), and
Saul of Tarsus (Acts 9:1–6; 22:6–16; 26:12–18).

The great lie—Often people receive the same news with different emotions. When someone celebrates a promotion, others are disappointed at being passed over. Disciples of Jesus rejoice that His prophetic words have come true. Previously Jesus had foretold, *"Behold, we are going up to Jerusalem; and the Son of man will be delivered to the chief priests and scribes, and they will condemn him to death, and deliver him to the Gentiles to be mocked and scourged and crucified, and he will be raised on the third day"* (Matthew 20:18–19). Everything happens exactly as Jesus predicted. The apostles rejoice, but the chief priests and elders are stunned by disastrous news. They watch the prophecies unfold, but they will not believe. They hear and see the same events as the disciples and crowds. Some believe, like the centurion. Others refuse and persist in unbelief, like the elders.

When the earth quaked the Lord rose again. Such miracles were done around the sepulchre that even the very soldiers who had come to guard it became witnesses, if they wanted to tell the truth. But the same avarice which made captive the disciple and companion of Christ made captive also the soldier who was on guard at the sepulchre. "We will give you money," they said, "and you can say that while you were sleeping His disciples came and took him away." . . . What is it that you have said, O unhappy cleverness? Have you so abandoned the light of the counsel of piety that you plunge into the depths of cunning and say this: "Say that while you were sleeping His disciples came and took Him away." You bring forward sleeping witnesses! Truly, you have yourself fallen asleep, who fall so greatly upon examination! If they were asleep, what could they see? And if they saw nothing, how are they witnesses?

    Saint Augustine of Hippo (AD 354–430), *Explanations of the Psalms*, 63, 15.

So, they fabricate a cover-up story. Chief priests bribe the guards to lie, and say that disciples stole Jesus' body while guards slept. Religious leaders become teachers of sin. Elders pay people to lie! Moreover, they concoct a lame and illogical story. If you were stealing a dead body, would you leave the burial clothes behind? And, if Jesus has not risen, the chief priests have a vested interest in finding that dead body, which they make no effort to seek. They *know* that Jesus has fulfilled His prophetic word. They don't even search for the corpse. Ironically, the story that the chief priests devise corroborates the accounts of all four evangelists in their Gospels—Jesus' tomb is empty! There is no dead body! Even today, many people put their faith in the evidence of the Resurrection and believe. Others prefer to believe the lie, persist in unbelief, or ignore this spectacular event altogether.

A Great Commission—is given to the eleven remaining apostles. Finally, they obey Jesus and proceed to Galilee to the mountain where they had been directed. They should have been there already. But, an angel and Jesus had to command them to get moving. Were they paralyzed with fear and disappointment? When the apostles see Jesus, they worship Him. But, some hesitate. How would you feel to meet someone you love, who was scourged, crowned with thorns, crucified, died, and left in a tomb for three days, standing in front of you? Shock, doubt, and hesitation seem to be normal reactions. What is happening here? How can this be?

Jesus came and said to them, "All authority in heaven and on earth has been given to me" (Matthew 28:18). The Resurrection of Jesus proves His authority as the Son of God, with power over everyone and everything. Jesus manifested His power by teaching (Matthew 5–7), healing the sick (Matthew 8–9), forgiving sins (Matthew 9:1–8), casting out demons (Matthew 8:28–32; 10:1), calming wind and storms at sea (Matthew 8:23–27), and raising the dead to life (Matthew 9:18–26). Now Jesus claims universal authority and shares His authority with His apostles.

Despite the human weakness displayed by His chosen apostles—who betray Him, deny Him, abandon Him in His hour of need, and hide in fear—Jesus remains constant. God has chosen these men to be apostles. Jesus is steadfast. Even when people are unfaithful, God remains faithful to His promises. Jesus gives a great commission and fourfold directive to His apostles:
+ Go
+ Make disciples of all nations
+ Baptize them in the name of the Father and of the Son and of the Holy Spirit
+ *Teach them to observe all that I have commanded you* (Matthew 28:19–20).

Jesus gives the Trinitarian formula for baptism—the sacrament of initiation into the Christian life. The Catholic Church recognizes as validly baptized, anyone who has been baptized with water using the words of Jesus from Matthew 28:19: "I baptize you in the name of the Father, and of the Son, and of the Holy Spirit." Jesus commands His followers to share the Good News with everyone, and leaves a comforting promise to His Church. *"Behold, I am with you always, to the close of the age"* (Matthew 28:20b). Amen. Stay with us, Lord. Come Lord Jesus!

1. What can you learn from the following passages?

Matthew 28:1–4
CCC 652
CCC 2174

2. What natural phenomenon can you find in these verses?

Matthew 27:51; 28:2
Revelation 6:12; 8:5

3. Who first went to the tomb and why?

Matthew 28:1
Mark 16:1
CCC 641

4. Describe the angel of the Lord and his message. Matthew 28:2–7

5. How did the soldiers guarding the tomb react? Matthew 28:4

6. What is the significance of the drama in Matthew 28:8–10?

CCC 640	
CCC 645	
CCC 654–655	

7. What sensory evidence in Matthew 28:9–10 proves that Jesus lives?

Sight	
Sound	
Touch	

8. Explain the drama in Matthew 28:11–15.

9. What objective sins do the leaders commit? Matthew 28:12–14, Leviticus 19:11

10. How do the chief priests inadvertently validate the truth of the Resurrection?

11. Who explains the Resurrection? Why is it important?

Acts 2:32–33
1 Corinthians 15:3–4
1 Corinthians 15:12–17

12. Where did the apostles go to meet Jesus after His Resurrection? Matthew 28:16

13. What did the disciples do when they saw Jesus?

Matthew 28:17
CCC 644

* What should you do? How can you do this? CCC 2096

14. Explain the source of Jesus' authority.

Matthew 28:18
Ephesians 1:20–22

15. Who is called to the kingdom of God? How must one respond? CCC 543

16. What does Jesus first command and what does this mean?

Matthew 28:19
CCC 232
CCC 730

17. Why did Jesus send the apostles out? CCC 1122

18. Explain the missionary mandate.

Matthew 28:19–20
CCC 1–2
CCC 850

19. What power does Jesus give the apostles? Matthew 18:19; CCC 1444

20. What does Jesus' promise and what does this indicate?

Matthew 28:20b
CCC 80

* What is the best thing you gained from your study of Matthew's Gospel?

Prayer Requests

Study the entire Catholic Bible

Catholic Bible Study

- Commentaries by world-renowned Catholic biblical scholars
- Suitable for a large parish Bible Study or for a small home group
- Children's Bible Study books for pre-school children
- DVD lectures available for each study

About Our Authors

Bishop Jan Liesen, SSD—wrote his dissertation on Sirach at the Biblicum, and was a member of the Papal Theological Commission. The author of *Wisdom* and *Mark*, he appears on many of our videos.

Bishop Michael Byrnes, STD—taught Scripture at Sacred Heart Seminary in Detroit after completing his doctorate in Rome. He collaborated on writing Romans, and appears on our videos.

Bishop Liesen, Dr. Manhardt, Bishop Byrnes

Father Ponessa

Father Joseph Ponessa, SSD—studied Scripture at the Biblicum, and is the primary author of *The Gospels of Matthew, Luke* and *John, Genesis, Moses and the Torah, David and the Psalms, Prophets and Apostles, Acts and Letters,* and many other books.

Laurie Watson Manhardt, PhD—the University of Michigan, wrote the commentaries on *Leviticus, Numbers, Psalms, Proverbs, Ecclesiastes, Wisdom, Judith, Esther, Romans, Philippians, Galatians, 1 and 2 Timothy, Titus,* and *1 and 2 Peter.*

Monsignor Charles Kosanke, STD—studied at the Pontifical Gregorian University in Rome, taught at Sacred Heart Seminary, and was rector of Saints Cyril and Methodius Seminary in Michigan. He is the primary author of *Isaiah.*

Monsignor Jan Majernik, STD—a native of Slovakia, earned a doctorate in Sacred Scripture from the Franciscan School of Biblical Studies in Jerusalem. He studied biblical archeology and biblical languages at the Hebrew University in Israel. He is the primary author of *The Synoptics.*

Father Andreas Hoeck, SSD—born in Cologne, Germany and earned his doctorate at the Pontifical Biblical Institute in Rome, where he wrote his dissertation on the book of Revelation. He is the author of *Ezekiel, Hebrews, Revelation.*

Sharon Doran, MA—studied Scripture at the Augustine Institute in Denver, and founded the Seeking Truth Bible Study in Omaha. Sharon wrote *Judges, Amos and Hosea* and appears on many videos.

Sharon Doran

Basic, Foundational Books

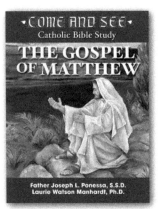

The Gospel of Matthew—The first book of the New Testament looks at the life and teachings of Jesus Christ in this 22 week study.

Genesis—Look at creation through the lens of science, and the lives of Adam and Eve, Noah, Abraham, Isaac and Jacob, in this 22 chapter study.

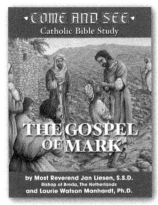

The Gospel of Mark—Study the first gospel written, recounting the life and ministry of Jesus in this 18 week study.

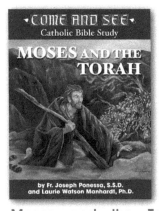

Moses and the Torah—Study *Exodus, Leviticus, Numbers*, and *Deuteronomy* in this 22 chapter book completing the Pentateuch.

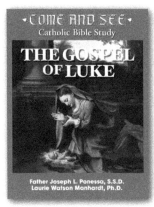

The Gospel of Luke—This 21 week study begins with the infancy narratives and early life of Jesus and continues to the Ascension of Our Lord.

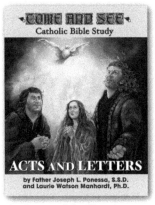

Acts and Letters—Explore the early Church through Luke's *Acts of the Apostles* and Paul's letters in this 22 week study.

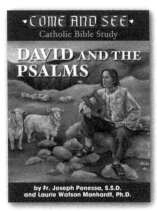

David and the Psalms—This 22 week study examines Ruth, Samuel and David, and their prayers—*Ruth, 1 and 2 Samuel, Psalms.*

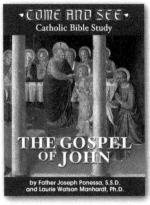

The Gospel of John—Study the life of Jesus from John's theological perspective, and see the sacraments emerge in this 21 week study.

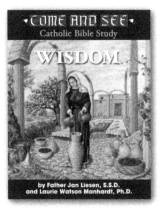

Wisdom—Bishop Liesen writes on the Wisdom literature of the Bible—*Job, Proverbs Song of Solomon, Wisdom, and Sirach.*

Advanced, Challenging Books

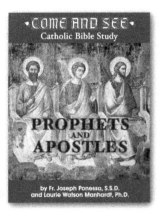

Prophets and Apostles—Old Testament prophets looked forward to God's promised Messiah while the New Testament apostles find fulfillment of prophecy in the life of Jesus.

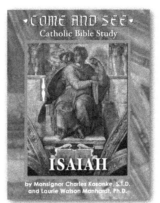

Isaiah—Called the fifth Gospel, this Old Testament prophet points to Jesus of Nazareth, the Suffering Servant and Redeemer of the world, in this 22 week study.

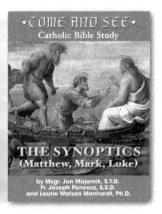

The Synoptics—Compare *Matthew, Mark,* and *Luke's* accounts of the life of Jesus as you journey through the Holy Land in this 22 week overview of the Gospels.

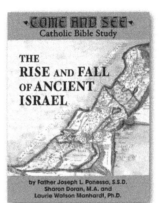

The Rise and Fall of Ancient Israel—Study the history of ancient Israel in this 21 week study of *Joshua, Judges, 1 and 2 Kings, 1 and 2 Chronicles, Amos, Hosea,* and *Jeremiah.*

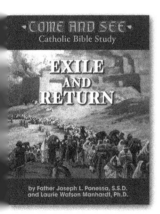

Exile and Return—*Tobit, Judith, Esther, Ezra, Nehemiah, 1 and 2 Maccabees* show how God worked in the lives of the Jewish people as they return to the Holy Land from the Babylonian exile.

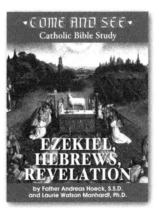

Ezekiel, Hebrews, Revelation — The Prophet Ezekiel has amazing visions similar to those of John revealed in the book of *Revelation. The Letter to the Hebrews* reveals Jesus the High Priest in this 22 week study.

www.CatholicBibleStudy.net   (772) 321-4034

www.EmmausRoad.org   (800) 398-5470   (740) 283-2880

Spanish Bible Studies

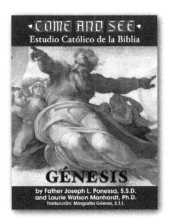

Endorsements

"The *Come and See ~ Catholic Bible Study* series provides an in depth and detailed analysis of the books of the Bible and is both an educational and spiritual way of approaching the word of God as revealed in Sacred Scripture."

Most Reverend Gerald M. Barbarito,
Bishop of Palm Beach, FL

"We found this Bible Study to be unique in several ways. It required personal preparation, reading the chapter and its excellent commentary provided by the authors, and answering questions that connected the chapter with other passages in the Old and New Testament and in the *Catechism of the Catholic Church*. The questions also invited us to personal reflection and to apply the teachings to our personal lives and to the problems of today. Thus, we learned a lot!"

Dr. and Mrs. Renato Gadenz, Eatontown, NJ

"The *Come and See ~ Catholic Bible Studies* are excellent and are helping men and women all over the country better understand the Bible and its relationship to the Catholic Church... Highly recommended."

Ralph Martin, S.T.D.,
President, Renewal Ministries, Ann Arbor
Director, New Evangelization,
Sacred Heart Seminary, Detroit, MI

"Certainly this is THE BEST study on the market. Not just because it is the least expensive, no, but, because it is so well done. I've researched extensively. It IS the best. Our parish is in the 10th year of *Come and See ~ Catholic Bible Study* and loving it!"

Chris Snyder,
Marlborough, MA

Come and See KIDS Books

Come and See KIDS is a Bible Study series written for pre-school to early elementary school age children. These companion books to the adult series could also be used alone.

- Bible memory verses and a Bible story
- Coloring pages illustrating the Bible story
- Craft activities for the child to make with a little bit of help

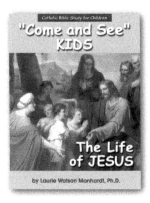

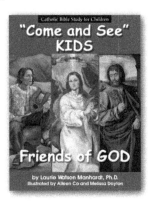

Emmaus Road Publishing
www.EmmausRoad.org
(800) 398-5470

Come and See ~ Catholic Bible Study
www.CatholicBibleStudy.net
(772) 321-4034

Seeking Truth Bible Study
www.SeekingTruth.net